The Conduct of Trial Cases with Some Suggestions on Examination-in-Chief, Cross-Examination and Re-Examination and Some Advice on Advocacy

Henry Juta

The Making of Modern Law collection of legal archives constitutes a genuine revolution in historical legal research because it opens up a wealth of rare and previously inaccessible sources in legal, constitutional, administrative, political, cultural, intellectual, and social history. This unique collection consists of three extensive archives that provide insight into more than 300 years of American and British history. These collections include:

Legal Treatises, 1800-1926: over 20,000 legal treatises provide a comprehensive collection in legal history, business and economics, politics and government.

Trials, 1600-1926: nearly 10,000 titles reveal the drama of famous, infamous, and obscure courtroom cases in America and the British Empire across three centuries.

Primary Sources, 1620-1926: includes reports, statutes and regulations in American history, including early state codes, municipal ordinances, constitutional conventions and compilations, and law dictionaries.

These archives provide a unique research tool for tracking the development of our modern legal system and how it has affected our culture, government, business – nearly every aspect of our everyday life. For the first time, these high-quality digital scans of original works are available via print-on-demand, making them readily accessible to libraries, students, independent scholars, and readers of all ages.

The BiblioLife Network

This project was made possible in part by the BiblioLife Network (BLN), a project aimed at addressing some of the huge challenges facing book preservationists around the world. The BLN includes libraries, library networks, archives, subject matter experts, online communities and library service providers. We believe every book ever published should be available as a high-quality print reproduction; printed on-demand anywhere in the world. This insures the ongoing accessibility of the content and helps generate sustainable revenue for the libraries and organizations that work to preserve these important materials.

The following book is in the "public domain" and represents an authentic reproduction of the text as printed by the original publisher. While we have attempted to accurately maintain the integrity of the original work, there are sometimes problems with the original work or the micro-film from which the books were digitized. This can result in minor errors in reproduction. Possible imperfections include missing and blurred pages, poor pictures, markings and other reproduction issues beyond our control. Because this work is culturally important, we have made it available as part of our commitment to protecting, preserving, and promoting the world's literature.

GUIDE TO FOLD-OUTS MAPS and OVERSIZED IMAGES

The book you are reading was digitized from microfilm captured over the past thirty to forty years. Years after the creation of the original microfilm, the book was converted to digital files and made available in an online database.

In an online database, page images do not need to conform to the size restrictions found in a printed book. When converting these images back into a printed bound book, the page sizes are standardized in ways that maintain the detail of the original. For large images, such as fold-out maps, the original page image is split into two or more pages

Guidelines used to determine how to split the page image follows:

• Some images are split vertically; large images require vertical and horizontal splits.
• For horizontal splits, the content is split left to right.
• For vertical splits, the content is split from top to bottom.
• For both vertical and horizontal splits, the image is processed from top left to bottom right.

THE
CONDUCT OF TRIAL CASES

WITH

SOME SUGGESTIONS ON EXAMINATION-IN-CHIEF, CROSS-EXAMINATION AND RE-EXAMINATION

AND

SOME ADVICE ON ADVOCACY

By

SIR HENRY JUTA

J. C. JUTA & CO.

Cape Town.   Johannesburg.   Port Elizabeth.

1919

THE RUSTICA PRESS
WYNBERG :: CAPE

CONTENTS.

SUBJECT.

CHAPTER I.

QUALIFICATION REQUIRED TO PRACTISE.

NEITHER IN the case of an Advocate nor of an Attorney is much time required for obtaining the qualification to practise. In the case of the former he is generally either called in one of the Inns of Court in England, or he is admitted in the Union after taking his Law Degree. There is no European country, I believe, where it was, and practically still is, such a simple matter to be called and admitted to the Bar as in England, and there is no profession in that Country for which a shorter time of reading is deemed requisite than that of a Barrister-at-Law. Three years, without the necessity of any other degree, with its fixed number of dinners to be eaten and its examinations—which the average man can hardly succeed in not passing—is all that is deemed necessary. Hence it is that so many holders of the Rhodes Scholarship, which lasts for three years, unless specially extended, enter this profession for which many have neither aptitude nor liking.

IN ENGLAND.

But for this short period of qualification there is some palliation in England. A man called to the Bar there would as soon think of actually practising without further qualification, as a youngster fresh from Sandhurst would think of commanding an

army on the Western Front. This necessary qualification he obtains by entering the Chambers of a practising Barrister and there for a year or two he learns
the practical side—also much of the theoretical for
that matter—of his profession. There he learns how
to handle a brief. He tries his "prentice" hand at
drawing pleadings, advising on evidence, etc., and
submits them to the Barrister whose pupil he is. In
time he is given a trial case to work up, and attends
the Court to watch the whole proceedings from start
to finish: indeed, he may even be entrusted with the
Brief as Junior in one Court while the Barrister is
occupied in some other Court. More than that; if he
has the capability he is often engaged for some years
more in "devilling" for some very busy Barrister,
before he thinks of starting Chambers on his own
account.

In England also there is some show of assurance
that the person seeking admission to practice is a fit
and proper person so far as character is concerned.
He requires the recommendation from two Benchers
of his Inn, and his application with some information
as to his parentage, etc., is screened: and if he comes
from any of the Colonies, Notice of his application
for call was screened in the Court of such Colony.
This allowed for due and proper objection being
made.

WITHIN THE UNION.

In this country anyone over twenty-one years, after
having passed the necessary examinations, is admitted to the Bar, and he proceeds to set up practising, without the slightest enquiry as to character,
and without any training or practice in the practical
side of his profession. What would be thought of it
if the Judges, or a deputed member of the Bench,

were to pay a "domiciliary visit" to the applicant as they did in Paris?

The question of taking pupils or "devils" was raised once or twice at the Cape Bar: but the decision come to was that, inasmuch as the population was small and the number of Advocates limited, such a course was undesirable—for reasons obvious to a Practitioner.

No practical experience.

The result naturally is that the Advocate beginning his career has very little, if any, idea of how to conduct a case, how to deal with witnesses, how to examine and cross-examine them, and how to avoid the dangers and pitfalls in which he may lose himself and his Client.

It is no answer to say that some South African intellectual giants have overcome these difficulties: average mankind does not consist of giants, intellectual or otherwise. No doubt a good deal can and should be learned by frequenting the Courts and watching the conduct of cases: but the average student spends the short period of three years in reading for his examinations, and finds no time for attending the Courts.

Practical fusion in case of attorneys.

With regard to Attorneys, what is really a new development has been created by the extended jurisdiction of Magistrates: and that is a practical fusion to some extent of the functions of the two professions. Under the old system the basis of pleadings was that they were verbal, and were in principle recorded by the Clerk of the Court: the pleadings therefore were never required by the Superior Courts to be judged of in the same way as pleadings in the latter Courts. Much latitude was allowed, especially as they were supposed to deal with simple cases involving small interests. The Jurisdiction has now been extended so as to include a large proportion of the cases which hitherto were tried in the Superior Courts, and the rules of pleadings follow for the most part the procedure which prevails there. It follows that the knowledge of the conduct of a case required of an Attorney, if he is to do justice to a Client, is very much greater now than under the old and limited jurisdiction. He is called upon now not only to do his *legitimate work as an Attorney,* but to perform all the functions which hitherto in the majority of cases were *performed by the Advocate in the Superior Courts.* Thus there has been a silent fusion of the functions of the professions. This was not of much importance under the old jurisdiction: it certainly is under the new.

The experience in South Africa with regard to the fusion of the professions is most undoubtedly against it. Apart from that consideration, which need not be pursued here, there are other objections. If, as I do not think can with reason be denied, three years are too short a time in which an Advocate can learn both the theoretical and practical sides of his profession, what is to be said of a system under which the practitioner is expected to become proficient not only as an Advocate but also as an Attorney within three years?

SERVICE OF ARTICLED CLERK TOO SHORT.

I do not suppose that many, if any, experienced men will be found who consider that the average articled Clerk is qualified to practise as an Attorney after being articled to an Attorney for three years. On the contrary I have no hesitation in saying that he is certainly not qualified. And with that I believe most of those experienced in both branches of the profession will agree. The time is too short for the Attorney to learn both the Law and practice of his profession. There is fortunately an examination to test the practical knowledge of a person seeking admission as an Attorney. How often does it not happen that such applicants are found quite unqualified to pass the practical test which has certainly not been of a very exacting nature hitherto. So much so is this the case, that new Rules have been framed at the request of the Cape Incorporated Law Society to put some limit to repeated and renewed applications for the practical examination by those who have failed to pass. The true cure for this evil is to extend the time beyond the three years of the Articles, which is too short.

Since writing the above the President of the Cape Incorporated Law Society has in his annual address enunciated similar views as to the term of the articles being too short.

RESULT OF EXTENDED JURISDICTION IN CASE OF ATTORNEYS.

That being so in the case of Attorneys, and the time being also too short in the case of Advocates, it is easy to imagine what the result will be where the Attorney is called upon under the extended jurisdiction of Magistrates to perform the functions both of Attorney and also those hitherto performed by Advocates. I imagine that one result will be partnerships, in which one partner does the work of the Attorney and another partner the work of Advocate: otherwise it is difficult to see how one man is to do the work expected of him with justice to his Client, or how while occupied all day in Court he is to attend to Clients who wish to consult him as an Attorney.

What the meaning of this is the public will discover before long.

In any case it would appear that some practical guidance as to Advocacy in the conduct of a case has become of even greater importance to the country practitioner than to the Junior Advocate. It is with that object in view that I have ventured to write the following practical suggestions in the hope that they may benefit not only the public who are the litigants, but that they may also help to lighten the labours of the Bench, whose onerous duties are certainly not lessened by the inexperience and want of the necessary qualifications of practitioners.

It will of course be understood by the reader that my remarks are generalizations. There are exceptions to all rules. When I deal with briefs which are delivered a few days before trial, it must not be supposed that there are not occasions on which they are delivered earlier, or when I generalize that material for cross-examination is not supplied, it must not be thought that there are not Attorneys who give most careful and exhaustive instructions on trial. There are: but I am referring to the general practice as I experienced it, which, as far as I can learn, is still the general practice.

Whether the following advice on examination and cross-examination will be of as little practical value as most " directions for use " when the reader tries to follow them for the first time, I tremble to think. I can only hope that some of it may spare the Junior bitter reflections and dark moments at the end of an unsuccessful trial case.

A few actual experiences are set out. In doing so there has been no desire to be egoistical. It has been done, not merely to illustrate my meaning, but to assure the reader that such advice as I venture to tender is not given ex cathedra, but as coming from one who has trodden the dusty and thorny road from Dan to Beersheba, eaten of the Dead Sea fruit and drunk of the Bitter Waters. The topography may be wrong and the metaphors mixed, but I can answer for the correctness of the sentiment.

———————

CHAPTER II.

SOME SUGGESTIONS FOR QUALIFICATION TO THE JUNIOR AND TO THE PRACTITIONER GENERALLY.

———

A very trying time for the Junior, especially if he be an industrious one, is the period between the taking of Chambers and the arrival of the Briefs. No doubt there are men who will continue conscientiously to read Law works and fill many note-books; but the average man longs for action, to put his reading to the test, and, indeed, to find an answer to the question he so often asks himself, whether he is really meant for the " rough and tumble " of the Bar, without which the Advocate cannot expect to succeed. There is so little room or opportunity for specialized or purely Chamber work. Nevertheless, this period of waiting is the golden and, perhaps, the only opportunity he will have of really obtaining some qualification for his profession.

Most students from South Africa who qualify in England, enter the Chambers of some experienced Barrister in good practice before returning home: if they are wise, they will most certainly do so. There they learn the practical part of the profession,—how to handle a brief, etc.

In this Country the Junior launches out into practice as soon as he is admitted without any preliminary training of any kind.

The only opportunity, therefore, which is afforded to the Junior of learning some of the practical side of his profession in this Country, is during that very period when he is waiting for Briefs. And it is not only the practical side which he should then learn, but the time may well be spent in properly qualifying himself in other directions. For it is absurd to imagine that the average man can become so in the three years required to pass the Examinations. It is quite true, and it is only right, that before being called to the Bar he is required to acquire some education, and therefore he has to graduate at the University. But unfortunately, I think, this education is now based on the " old classical and historical system " of England. The man taking his degree " specializes (!) " in some branch or other ; either on what is called the classical side or the mathematical or some other side. And here it may be noted that few Mathematicians have distinguished themselves as Lawyers. The senior wranglers in England who have become at all celebrated at the Bar could be counted on one hand. This may seem curious, as the basis of Mathematics is logical deduction. The reason for this is, I believe, that a great Lawyer is distinguished by an uncommon amount of common sense. The perusal of the Judgments of great Judges will at once show the reader the shrewd common sense grip with which they apply the principles of Law.

The erudition of a scholar in what is generally called the Classics, viz., Latin and Greek, is not of much assistance to the Jurist. It was not always the case that a Graduate had to " specialize." In former days the knowledge required for a degree may not have been by any means so deep or thorough as nowadays, but it was certainly no bad education for the

Bar: for it was in that kind of knowledge that were trained de Villiers, R. Solomon, J. Leonard, the present Chief Justice, W. Solomon, the two Maasdorps, Kotzè, Schreiner and Searle.

The acquisition of an erudition in the Greek particles to the neglect, *inter alia,* of modern languages, seems rather a waste of time for a profession other than the scholastic one: whereas for the Jurist it is very necessary that he should know, besides the Latin language, also Dutch, French and German. It may be said that men can get on, and have successfully done so, without being able to read these languages: but so they have without any knowledge of Conic Sections or a Chorus in Euripides or Sophocles. It is surely better for the Advocate to be able to read and digest the authorities in our Law, which are in Latin, Dutch, French and German, putting aside the educational value of the Literature of these languages. The difficulties, therefore, that meet the South African at the threshold of his profession are only too real, and more numerous than those which the man practising in England has to contend with. He sometimes reads books which profess to give advice on the practical side of his profession, how to qualify himself, and how to deal with witnesses and cases in Court. I have also in my time read some, and confess that they were of very little assistance, if any. They are either too theoretical when written by one who has not been through the mill, or they are too advanced, too technical.

May I venture to give the young practitioner some practical advice on the best way of filling up that trying time when he is waiting for Briefs or Clients.

THE USE OF THE VOICE.

1. If he has not already done so during his years of reading, then do let him pay some attention to learning *how to use his voice*. This seems to me to be the most neglected side of the profession: quite as sadly neglected as among preachers. If a boy is fluent and glib of speech, that is all that is deemed necessary. How many take the trouble to learn elocution: very few, indeed. But elocution is by no means the only thing required. One may hear clever Elocutionists—when seated among the front rows: but go to the back of the Hall, and you cannot hear half of what they are saying. What is as much to be aimed at as clear speaking and a power of modulation is a knowledge of the necessary *pitch*. The Junior of to-day cannot hear a Thomas Upington, who was a wonderful example of control of pitch of voice. Whether in Court or in the House, no matter how physically ill he was, his voice always reached to the ends of the place he was speaking in, and was never unduly or unnecessarily loud. But he might, with great benefit to himself in more ways than one, go and hear the Dean of Cape Town in the pulpit, or Creswell in the House of Assembly. The inexperienced speaker thinks that the louder he shouts the better he can be heard: to a certain extent that is true, he may be *heard;* but the object aimed at by a speaker is much more than that,—it is to be *listened* to. And it is a question whether it is more trying to be shouted at or to strain the ears trying to hear. Yet every speaker must have noticed that the " stage whisper " carries further and more clearly than many of the Actors' natural voices. It is a matter of pitch. It may come naturally: but that is rare. The trouble and training required was brought home by a young American Lawyer, ambitious also for Parliamentary

honours. He would go with a fidus Achates into every Hall or large building in London to which he could obtain permission, simply for the purpose of estimating the pitch and testing its correctness.

When it comes to trying his persuasive seductiveness on a Jury, some of whom are holding their hands up to their ears in order to hear the speaker, while others show visible signs of painful headache or earache, the practitioner will begin to wish that he had some knowledge of the carrying capacity of a properly pitched voice.

KNOWLEDGE OF DUTCH, LATIN, FRENCH AND GERMAN.

2. The authorities in our Law are written in English, Dutch, French, German and Latin. Most of those in French, and a few written in German, are translated into English. But there is no doubt that a knowledge of these languages is a great help to the Jurist. Unfortunately the graduate in Law is handicapped by the "Classical or Historical" system adopted in our University, and few Advocates have had an education in modern languages. It is of little use suggesting that the Junior should acquire a reading knowledge of French and German. One feels that it is too late: these languages should have been learnt at School and College.

A knowledge of Dutch is very necessary, and so is that of the colloquially spoken language in South Africa. This latter is a very great help indeed in dealing with witnesses both in and out of Court. Every practitioner should, even if he cannot read the Dutch authorities, make himself acquainted with colloquially spoken Dutch.

The Latin of the civilians and text-book writers differs somewhat from Classical Latin: but it is readily dealt with after a little practice. Many men have found it not only a help to them in their profession, but in more immediate ways, to translate into English some Latin work of a well-known authority. When the practitioner relies on and cites long passages from authorities in Latin and often in Dutch, he should have translations ready: it is sometimes more difficult to follow old Law Dutch than Latin.

KNOWLEDGE OF ACCOUNTANCY.

3. I have often heard numbers of the Mercantile community complain of the want of knowledge of book-keeping—even of the most elementary kind—shown by the average practitioner. The complaint is only too well founded. But it is not brought home to the young practitioner that such knowledge should form part of his training. It certainly was not in my salad days.

It may be of interest to relate the experience of a young practitioner which resulted in his learning some Accountancy, which was of the greatest help to him in his profession. It certainly was not learnt by reason of any inspired forethought. He was briefed as Junior in one of the Letterstedt cases, involving complicated accounts. The litigation between the heirs in that estate and the board of Executors, as Executors and administrators, had been proceeding for some time before he joined the Bar, so that he knew nothing about it, and in relating his experience he did not hesitate to confess that he could make very little, if anything, of the mass of accounts and documents in the Brief. A Consultation was fixed with the two Accountants for the heirs, Messrs. W. G. Steytler and George Cosnett. Both were very clever and experienced men in their professions: but for what may be called " Detective Accountancy," that is for unravelling accounts of set purpose made to represent other than the actual facts, George Cosnett was unrivalled.

The consultation duly took place, but as the Senior could not attend, it fell to the Junior's lot to receive the Accountants' report and advise (!) thereon. He listened attentively, but it was soon borne upon him that for all the good he was doing, he might as well not have been there. Something had to be done "to save face," as the Chinese say. Now there was a globular sum of £14,000 which kept recurring again and again, so it was selected in desperation, and the Junior said with perfect sincerity that he did not understand it. Steytler, in a kindly manner, began to explain it, but there was a slightly patronising air about the explanation—and no wonder—which was transparently much too technical for the Junior—so Cosnett interrupted and began to enlighten him in simple language. "No, Cosnett," broke in Steytler, "you are putting it all wrong." "Wrong!" shouted the impetuous George, "I tell you it is so." This was the Junior's opportunity. "Mr. Fairbridge," he said, "we had better adjourn this consultation until the Accountants are agreed as to the figures!" With that he took up his hat and brief and walked out, leaving Steytler and Cosnett in a hot discussion.

It turned out that there was something very wrong with this item, but the full extent of what this meant he did not realize until a leading firm of Merchants asked him to arbitrate between the partners on the state of their accounts. Now the fat was in the fire. To save it, all the fees earned for some time thereafter were paid to Cosnett to teach him Book-keeping, and a most useful thing he found it.

Every Junior is strongly advised to learn Book-keeping, and if he will take the time and trouble to master some Accountancy as well, he will find this "hint" a very "valuable" one, when his proficiency becomes known, as undoubtedly it will.

But if some knowledge of Accountancy is required in an Advocate, how much more essential is it that the Attorney should have such knowledge. The latter receives and deals with *other people's moneys* in various ways: and it too often happens that they are *mixed up with his own,* sometimes with very *sad results.* Is it too much to say—I do not think so—that some Attorneys have muddled their affairs and messed their careers, not through any deviation from the straight and narrow path, but entirely from ignorance of the proper application of the essential principle—" die geld ontvangt, een schuldenaar, die geld betaalt, een crediteur": " Who receives money is Debtor: who pays it is Creditor." I have heard a well-known and experienced Banker declare that every Attorney should be compelled to pass an Examination in Accountancy as a necessary qualification before being admitted to practice. With this opinion I wholly concur. Accountancy to the Attorney is certainly a greater necessity than a smattering of Roman Law.

4. SHORTHAND.

Proficiency in Shorthand will be found very useful to the Junior, because it opens other ways of bringing grist to the mill: to the Attorney because it saves valuable time in taking instructions and statements, especially to the beginner who cannot afford a large staff.

5. CONSULT THE SENIORS.

And, lastly, this advice to the Junior. He will find that his older and more experienced brethren at the Bar will always be ready and willing to give him any help or assistance possible. He need, therefore, never hesitate when he is in difficulty and doubt to call on one of the leading Advocates for advice. Let me give an illustration of the way in which the thorny path of inexperience may be made easier. For the first day of my debut in the Supreme Court I was briefed, as was customary, with some " Confirmations of Accounts in Insolvent Estates "—the so-called "Similar Motion." The first brief was in an estate which was a fairly bulky portfolio. I had not the faintest notion what to do with it. A visit of five minutes to a Senior would have taught me what an elementary Motion it was: but I did not know that such a course was open to me. Hours were spent over that brief: all the figures were counted up: the vouchers were compared with the accounts and checked: and at the end of all this work I was no wiser than before. Fortunately there were several of these Motions called before the first one briefed to me was reached, so that I was able to grasp the arduous duty to be performed and move " Similar Motion My Lord." But what unnecessary misery would have been spared me, if I had only asked a Senior what to do. If the Junior has, through inexperience, doubts and difficulties, let him seek the Counsel of a Senior and he will receive sympathetic and helpful advice.

NERVOUSNESS.

A knowledge of what to do, how to handle the brief, and the like will go far to give the Junior some self-confidence and to combat the usual nervousness.

Some even worry terribly over the latter. This should not be allowed to be exaggerated. When once in the battle it is marvellous how it disappears. Many very good Advocates never get over the feeling at the opening of the case: even after years of experience they feel on the first day of the new Term as if they were at the very threshold of their career. After the first few moments, their nerves are under control.

———————

CHAPTER III.

ADVOCACY.

———

SAID ONE Bridge player to another: "I am just about even at the end of the year." Said the other, a good player, who had studied the game and its rules: "I make a few hundred a year." "Then you must be an uncommonly lucky holder of cards," laughed the first man. "Not at all," replied the other, "I hold no better or worse cards than you do. But I make the most of my good cards: and when I have bad ones, I minimise my losses. The result is that I am a winner by the end of the year." A successful Advocate appears to be very much in the position of the winner at Bridge: he makes the most of good material: and when he has a bad case, he minimises the loss. Outside novels, in which the Hero, the Advocate, throws all the rules of evidence to the winds with the acquiescence of a complacent Judge and without objection from the Prosecutor, ignorant of the elementary rules of Law and practice, miracles do not happen in the Law Courts any more than in any other place on our globe. But what does happen and not at all infrequently is that a good case is lost by bad advocacy: and cases are won, not through the merits of the successful pleader but owing to the blunders of his opponent. Brilliancy in cross-examination alone will not suffice. Of course one hears it said, "So and So made the witnesses say just what he pleased; we did not stand a chance." The writer is not a believer in the idea that a cross-examiner can make a witness who saw that a thing was black say that it was white. What he can elicit from the witness is that the blackness was not so deep as the latter stated in Examination in Chief: that there was a good deal of white in it: that it was really a grey, and that in the existing light and surrounding circumstances, it might well be taken for white. But even that will not avail unless he makes the most of his own material to establish the fact that the thing was white. There is no doubt also that a clever address to a Jury will go a long way to ensure a verdict: but the greatest factor after all in Advocacy is to make the most of his good cards, and when they are bad so that he cannot win, to minimise the loss to his Client as much as possible. And he may have as bad a run of losing cases as a cardplayer has of bad luck. A whole term may pass without his being briefed in any but losing cases, a most trying and desponding time for the beginner, whether he be Counsel or an Attorney practising in the Magistrate's Court.

The first and main principle for the practitioner therefore is to make the most of his own materials and to present his case in the best manner possible.

CHAPTER IV.

TRIAL BY JURY.

———

A. IN CIVIL CASES.

THE RIGHT to demand a trial by Jury in a Civil case does not prevail throughout the Union: it is confined to certain Provinces. The more one sees of such trials the more convinced one becomes that it was a mistake to allow them. It is not the case in such trials, as in suits before a Judge or Magistrate, of making the most of one's material before trained men who are accustomed to weigh evidence: it is the case of arousing and working on the bias, prejudices, sympathy and emotions of ordinary and untrained men.

WHEN TRIAL BY JURY IS USUALLY DEMANDED.

Either party may demand a trial by Jury after the pleadings are closed, and the Junior may be called upon to advise whether or not the case shall be heard by a Judge, or by a Judge and Jury. If the opponent is the Government, or a Corporation, or a man well-known to be rich, or an unpopular person, or there is some passing popular feeling against him as one of a class, or if the Client is a popular hero, politically or otherwise, then a trial by Jury is demanded.

In the case of a Criminal trial, where such popular and political feelings, or public prejudice for or against a prisoner prevail, the trial can be and is removed to some other place, on the ground that a fair and impartial trial cannot take place in the Town or District where such feelings are rampant. In a civil case, that is the very ground seized on as the reason for demanding a trial by Jury. Which demonstrates what a mistake it is in Civil cases.

If the Client be a humble widow or orphan or a poor man fighting a rich one and the practitioner has to rely on "sympathy" to succeed, a Jury is demanded.

If the widow be smart or at all notorious, it may be a question whether or not to avoid a Jury. No practitioner in my opinion, can possibly tell what will influence a Jury: and as there are sure to be some married men among them, their wives will have no sympathy with the "hussy," and all the warnings of the Judge that the Jury must not discuss the case with any outsider will not prevent those wives from saying what *they* think of "The Lady in the case." The unmarried practitioner may not appreciate the effect of the widow being smart or notorious upon the verdict: the married Jurors may.

DAMAGES A LEGITIMATE GROUND.

A legitimate ground for claiming a trial by Jury is where substantial damages are desired. There can be no doubt that there was a feeling in the profession that the Court did not award adequate damages, and that the amount ordered to be paid to the successful Plaintiff was often not sufficient even to cover the costs between Attorney and Client, and that this feeling was the reason for the Legislation on this matter. I remember a case years ago—Eheu! fugaces! which certainly accentuated the feeling. A large firm dealing extensively in buying South African produce was accused by the Defendant of using weights which were not true and correct. A libel action followed in due course and the firm won: but the Court, holding that the Plaintiff had come into Court more for the purpose of vindicating its character than for damages, *awarded £5 damages and Magistrate's Court costs.*

Whether Magistrates are likely to be more liberal in the way of damages—and their jurisdiction is now fairly large—may be doubted. Trial by Jury in the Magistrate's Court in civil cases cannot take place: but provision is made in Section 34 of Act 32 of 1917 for assessors, from which some interesting developments may be expected.

WHAT IS THE PRACTITIONER TO DO IF HE BE ON THE UNSYMPATHETIC SIDE.

The chances of securing a verdict in your Client's favour in such a case are very remote. In the conduct of a case therefore, where the Client is in a pecuniary position which will enable him to appeal, *this ultimate appeal* must be kept well before the practitioner.

THE ADVICE SUGGESTED APPLIES NOT ONLY TO THE CASE OF A TRIAL BY JURY BUT TO AN APPEAL FROM THE MAGISTRATE'S COURT.

Although the suggestions about to be offered fall under the heading of " Jury Trials," they apply also where it is intended to appeal from the Magistrate's decision and some of the comments are really more applicable in the latter case.

There are generally speaking two points, in regard to which *the case should be conducted with a view to the Appeal Court.*

1. MIXED LAW AND FACT.

The first is where the matter is one of mixed Law and Fact. There is little hope of the appellant suc-

ceeding in reversing the finding of fact by either the
Jury or the Magistrate. But in a mixed case of Law
and Fact, the question is often whether the facts are
sufficient to support the conclusion of Law. Thus the
action may be for damages caused by the negligence
of the Defendant. To constitute such negligence a
considerable number of facts are often necessary.
With these clearly before him, the practitioner
must be careful that *all* the facts on which *he* will
rely against the conclusions of negligence are brought
out. Let me illustrate by a simple case. How often
may the following sort of evidence not be found in
records: " when I saw the accident I was standing at
the corner of Russel and Regent Streets:" " It was
about as far away as the park is from here"—and that
is all. Of course the Magistrate and the Practitioners
and everybody concerned know where Russel and
Regent Streets are, and where the Park is, and so no
one troubles to define the locality. The locality and
the distance, however, must be of materiality or the
questions would never have been put. But the
Appeal Court knows nothing of the locality or the
distance, and so the force and effect of the evidence,
so apparent and obvious to the practitioner himself,
is lost. Sometimes the Magistrate adds something
explanatory to the evidence: but many do not, and
it is the business of the practitioner to get the
evidence properly recorded. Sometimes the explanation is recorded by a distance being given in
brackets: thus after the latter answer will be found
e.g. " (30 yards)". Even so it is not clear whether
this is the Magistrate's estimate or the evidence of
the witness.

Now this may seem a trival matter. Yes! and yet
how often is not this elementary blunder committed:
and ex uno disce—I will not say all, but a good

many mistakes. Therefore the practitioner must be careful that all the facts upon which the appeal is to be based, e.g., on the ground that the evidence does not amount to negligence, are properly brought out and proved. The opposite party will have to see that all *his* facts are recorded: it is not for the practitioner to assist him. If the question of the distance or the locality is part of *his* case, do not misunderstand these comments to mean that you, who are for the Defendant, must get the distances and locality defined. It is only when it is material for *your* appeal to have them defined, that you should see that the evidence is both given and recorded. Take nothing therefore for granted: indeed, in all trials before a Jury the practitioner should take nothing for granted, because in my opinion no one can say what may not influence a Juror.

2. OBJECTIONS TO INADMISSIBLE EVIDENCE, ILLEGALITIES AND IRREGULARITIES.

The next point to which the attention of the practitioner should be directed *with a view to appealing* is the *objection to inadmissible evidence, and to illegalities or irregularities in procedure.*

Where the trial by Jury in a civil case is one not based upon such bias, prejudice, etc., as has been referred to, so that your Client will have a fair hearing, it is not advisable to raise many objections to the admission of evidence. Even if such objections are perfectly legitimate, your opponent will in some way or other convey to the Jury that an attempt is being made to stifle the statements of witnesses which would be in favour of his client, "and if they could—they would—etc." It is only another instance of working on the prejudices, sympathy, etc., of men, who are quite unable to appreciate the necessity of the admission of evidence being governed by rules.

Now I am not referring to trivial and unimportant objections, even if legally sound. Because even on appeal, the fact that evidence was admitted which was inadmissible will not affect the result, if the evidence was not both on a material point and prejudicial.

In a civil Jury trial, where your Client is the unsympathetic party, there *is no need to pay the same attention to the feelings of the Jury*: your object is to keep the Appeal Court in view, and therefore all objections of substance to the admission of inadmissible evidence should be properly taken and requested to be recorded.

3.   THE AMOUNT OF DAMAGES.

The third point is the question of damages. The Appeal Court has jurisdiction to reduce the damages, and as Juries are prone to give a large sum as damages, this is one of the few directions in which it is possible to get some relief for your Client—if you are on the unsympathetic side.

TENDERS IN CIVIL JURY TRIALS.

It often becomes important in these trials to consider whether or not to *make a tender*. Where your Client is the "unsympathetic" one, it is the result of my experience that a tender made with a view of saving costs is of little avail, if any. I remember a case against the Government during the time the plague raged in Cape Town. Various premises were thoroughly cleaned out, and of necessity damage was caused. An action to recover such damage was brought. At the most extravagant and liberal estimate £25 would have been sufficient compensation:

but as the Plaintiff had no means to pay the costs the sum of £100 was tendered in the hope that thus the costs of the trial might be avoided. The Jury were just about to retire, when one of them rose and asked the Judge if a verdict for £100 would give the Plaintiff his costs. He was told that the latter would get his costs only up to the date of tender. The result was a verdict for £150. The motives of the Jury were only too apparent.

It is better to pay the money into Court: but even in that case the Jury will be aware of the payment, if it has to be pleaded: though it may not strike them with the same force as a tender.

While the right to demand a trial by Jury in Civil cases continues to exist, it would certainly conduce to the Administration of Justice, if pleadings, etc., could so be arranged that the Jury is *not* made acquainted with the fact either that a tender or a payment into Court has been made.

CHAPTER V.

INSPECTION OF THE LOCUS IN QUO.

———

THE INSPECTION of the locus in quo, when the topographical features and the like are elements in the case, is of the very greatest use at this stage. That is, an inspection made on behalf of your Client *before the trial,* when you can be accompanied by the principal witnesses on your side. It enables Counsel to examine his witnesses in a clear and intelligible manner,—*a matter of vital importance,* not only to them, but also to the Bench. The only danger which Counsel should be on guard against after such inspection is that of dealing with the case as if the Judge or the Jury are equally well acquainted with the locality, which may lead him into neglecting to have all the necessary facts recorded. He is by the inspection able to visualize the scene when in Court, and may in consequence omit to elicit some fact which seems quite unnecessary to have evidence upon; because knowing all the positions, distances, etc., such fact must, in his mind, necessarily follow from what has already been deposed to. It becomes self-evident to him : but it may not be so to a person who has to construct the scene from the oral testimony of other eye-witnesses. With this precaution well before him, there is no question of the utility of such an inspection.

It enables the practitioner to cross-examine.

It moreover enables him to deal very much more effectually with the witnesses on his opponent's side. When a would-be-knowing witness against you puts on an air of superiority and says with a condescending smile or sneer at your ignorance, "you would not put such" (here follows a slight pause which is intended to be filled up by the word "silly" or something stronger) "questions if you were acquainted with the locality," the riposte "that is just what I am Mr. —" transfers the "silliness," etc., to his side.

The inspection should take place as early as possible before the Advice on Evidence.

This inspection should take place as early as possible in the course of the action, instead of being left, as it so often is, to the last moment. I know nothing more annoying than to find, when you visit the locus in quo, that something which was not appreciated from a perusal of papers or not sufficiently so, either by yourself or by others on your side, has an important bearing on the case, and that there is no time to make proper enquiries and follow them up: the more so when you find in Court that your opponents have not overlooked it, and are "barraging in" their version for all they are worth without your being able to stem the attack in any way.

On Circuit.

An inspection cannot therefore take place too early. On Circuit this of necessity must be at the last moment if the case is coming on at that sitting. But wise and experienced litigants in the country—and there are not a few such, e.g., in "Water Zaken"—take the precaution to get their Counsel to make the inspection at the Circuit sitting prior

to the one at which the case is to come on: or if the
case is to be heard in Cape Town an inspection is
arranged for during the Circuit Sitting prior to the
date of trial. It is sometimes impossible to estimate
the value of such an inspection on behalf of the
Client.

INSPECTION DURING THE COURSE OF THE TRIAL.

Very different in its nature, objects and value is
an inspection made during the trial.

It sometimes happens that an inspection is suggested *in Court* in the course of the trial: and here
it behoves Counsel to be wary and circumspect. I
was no great lover when at the Bar of such inspec-
tions, notwithstanding the opinions expressed in the
books as to the great weight to be attached to visual
evidence. There was in my humble opinion too much
danger of the Judge or Jury deciding the issues upon
their impressions of the locality and *not upon the
evidence.* A casual inspection of such a nature differs toto coelo from one in which you are accompanied by your own witnesses, to whom you can be
putting questions all the time. It generally means,
especially in the case of a Jury trial, that a regular
posse of people, Judge, Jury, Counsel, and Attorneys
and their Clerks spread themselves over the locus in
quo: and every Juror is too liable to form impressions from his casual inspection, and to depend upon
his own judgment. If they were all persons skilled
in the knowledge of the circumstances of the particular case, it might be different. But they are not all
necessarily such: some are certain not to be. Now a
long acquaintance with the topography of a locality,
etc., is a very different thing from a casual walk over
the ground. Levels are by no means what they often
appear to the eye to be: soils which appear a sandy

waste, are not necessarily so: and rich-looking loam may be in fact less cultivable than dry-looking stuff: and so on. The Juror sees the sandy soil, and thereafter in Court smiles at the experienced witness who testifies that it is better than the black rich-looking loam. He, in short, cannot even *gauge* the value of the evidence by his inspection: and he is much more likely to *weigh* it in accordance with his own opinion.

Be Careful of Offers of Inspection.

These remarks apply to both parties to a suit: nevertheless offers of an inspection are made and urged by one or other side in trial cases. When made by your opponent the question arises whether they are to be accepted or not. It is obvious that a refusal is bound to create a bad impression: for it suggests to the Jury that you are afraid to let them test the correctness of your witnesses' statements by visual testimony. If you have not seen the locality yourself, the difficulty of judging is naturally greatly increased. The offer may be merely "bluff," made for the very purpose of creating this impression: it may on the other hand be made genuinely. It is also obvious that one cannot give advice of practical value to a person fighting in the dark. Where your case depends upon expert or skilled evidence, or experience, the inspection from your point of view cannot be of much material assistance. In such cases what happens is that Counsel, while not declining the inspection—to do so *directly* is bad advocacy, no matter how legitimate the declining might be—emphasizes as strongly as possible that for the above reasons the inspection is more likely to be misleading than of real assistance in arriving at the truth. In other cases you may welcome the offer, especially when you know the locality. If it was a "bluff" the "biter is bit."

CHAPTER VI.

*

ADVICE ON EVIDENCE.

———

AFTER THE pleadings have been closed, and very often along with the brief for drawing the final pleading, Counsel is briefed to advise on evidence.

ABSENCE OF INSTRUCTIONS.

In the majority of cases the instructions for this advice are limited to the pleadings; sometimes, the instructions upon which the declaration or plea is founded accompany the Brief, in which case some idea of the persons who can give evidence can be obtained. But rarely, indeed, is Counsel briefed with the statements of the witnesses relied upon by the client to support his case. The reason for this seems to arise from the fact, that should the case be settled before the advice is acted upon, or should Counsel conclude that any of the persons whose statements have been taken should not be called, the costs consequent upon taking and briefing the statements may or will not be allowed.

CAUSED BY CONSIDERATION OF COSTS.

This question of the allowance or disallowance of the costs of witnesses will meet Counsel in all the steps necessary in calling witnesses. It is one naturally of great importance to the Client. To Counsel the primary factor is that the latter should win his case: but it will be little satisfaction to him if the victory should prove a Pyrrhic one, if the costs not recoverable from the losing side should be so great as to make the Judgment one not worth obtaining. And herein lies the difficult responsibility of Counsel: to obtain all the information and evidence necessary for the success of the action without mulcting the successful Client in paying costs out of his own pocket. The latter consideration is of course one of vital importance to the Attorney in the case. The result follows that, *as a general rule*, Counsel in advising on the evidence to be called has nothing before him but the pleadings: that is, he simply has before him the issues of fact in dispute as disclosed on the pleadings.

NEW RULE SHOULD OBVIATE SOME OF THE DIFFICULTY.

Under the Rules lately framed by the Court it is provided that the Taxing Officer may allow the Attorney of the successful party a sum in his discretion, not exceeding 25 guineas, for services rendered by the Attorney in the way of necessary preparation or enquiry made prior to the institution of the suit or enquiry made during its course for the necessary purposes thereof. This rule should enable Counsel to have something more before him than the mere issues in the pleadings.

STATEMENTS OF WITNESSES.

In the later years of my practice I often requested to be supplied with the statements of the witnesses relied upon by the Client *before advising on evidence*: but the beginner, I am afraid, will have to be satisfied with the Pleadings and some instructions. Sometimes, Clients are so neglectful of their own interests, or the regard for the saving of costs is carried to such an extreme, that the Brief to advise on evidence is not delivered *until* the case is set down for trial. I have even heard this, viz.: that Counsel had not been briefed to advise on evidence before notice of trial, advanced in Court as a *reason* for asking the Court to extend the set down of the case to a later date. The reason was, however, obvious. The Plaintiff was a poor man, and the Defendant was afraid of incurring the costs of briefing the advice on evidence unless it was certain that the case would come on: for although such costs are taxable as between party and party, it did not follow that the Plaintiff was in a position to pay them even should he not proceed to trial. It is obvious that the period between the notice of trial and the trial was much too short for the advice to be of any practical value. If the Court refused to extend the time, then the Defendant ran the very real risk of coming into Court with not even a "half-baked" case: which means that the chances of success were all against him. But such are the ways of Clients and the difficulties of the Practitioner.

The best way of preparing a case for trial is *first* to submit the proofs of witnesses to Counsel: *next* to hold an inspection of the locus in quo (on which see p. 27): and then for the advice on evidence to be given.

THE OBVIOUS COURSE IS OF LITTLE PRACTICAL VALUE.

It is very simple in such cases to advise that evidence should be called upon the issues raised on the pleadings and upon the points of Law involved therein which require foundations of fact. But that will not be of much practical value, and will go a very little way in obtaining Judgment in the Client's favour. Something more is obviously required: the question is what is that something.

THE COURSE SUGGESTED.

In considering the issue of fact which is alleged on one side and denied on the other it is well to remember the following:

1. WITNESSES DO NOT OFTEN DELIBERATELY COMMIT PERJURY.

Witnesses seldom come into the Witness-box to deliberately commit perjury: but owing to bias, prejudice, forgetfulness, etc., their evidence is exaggerated or distorted.

2. CLIENTS CONCEAL OR RESERVE MATERIAL FACTS.

Clients very often conceal or reserve mentioning some fact or facts relevant to the case even from their own advisers: sometimes, because they consider them to be of no importance; often through some strange process of reasoning that if unknown to their own Counsel, the facts will be unknown to the opposite party and will never be disclosed—sometimes however this is done deliberately by clients where the disclosure might show that they have no case: for there is no reason to suppose that the truth necessarily lies with your Client.

3. OPPOSITE PARTY NOT RISKING COSTS FOR NOTHING.

That the opposite party is not incurring the costs of the action without having, at least, some show in his favour.

THE DANGER OF AN APPARENTLY CLEAR CASE.

With regard to the latter point, the practitioner cannot be too seriously warned to be on his guard when his case appears so clear, that neither the Client nor his Attorney " can see how they can possibly lose

the case," or both confidentially ask "what in the
world is the Defendant contesting the case for." The
more certain your case seems, and the more inex-
plicable the conduct of the other side in coming into
Court, the more assured you may be that either your
Client is concealing something, or that things are
not what they seem, and that a very unpleasant surprise and rude awakening is waiting for you in
Court,—unless you realize this position.

LOOKING AT THE CASE FROM THE OPPONENT'S VIEW.

This should also induce the Junior to look very
carefully into the legal position. A most valuable
gift to an Advocate is the capability of "looking all
round a case," and one of the most successful men
at the Bar I have known, was he who, although perhaps not as great a Jurist as some others, had the
faculty of seeing the other side of a case. One is too
apt to see only one's Client's side, and to devote one's
research to his side of the controversy—a fault which
applies to evidence as well as to purely legal questions. One of the best fights put up on a losing
side was in a Motion of some importance in which
the Counsel conceived the erroneous impression that
he was appearing for the Applicant instead of the
Respondent, and he received a cruel shock when he
rose to appear for the former and found his opponent
doing the same. But he found that he was in a better
position to point out the weakness of the Applicant's
case than if he had devoted himself to the strength
of his own.

BRIEFING AT THE LAST MOMENT.

Unfortunately owing to the practice prevailing of
not briefing Counsel until the last moment there is
little time to approach and look at the case from

your opponent's view. In England, when I was in Chambers, Briefs were delivered weeks, and even months, before the day of hearing: here, one was fortunate if the *complete* Brief was delivered several days before. If it were otherwise Counsel could, if he has not the rare faculty of " looking all round the case," devote some time to getting up the Brief as if he were on the opposing side. But as things are the result is that surprises are sometimes sprung upon him—and not always the Junior either,—of points of Law which have not been foreseen or anticipated.

BEWARE THEREFORE OF WHAT APPEARS A " CERTAINTY."

The more certain therefore the case for his Client looks the more the practitioner should try to guard against some such surprise; there may be none; but it is a safe test to apply in such cases that the opposing side is not incurring the expense of litigation without having some show in his favour. What that something is, Counsel must try to discover. And this, as I have said, applies as well to questions of evidence as to points of law.

TRY TO CONCEIVE THE DEFENDANT'S CASE.

In advising on evidence, therefore, it is well to try to conceive for yourself what, upon the state of the pleadings and such instructions as you may have, the case of the Defendant may be. This will be found of great use also when it comes to the cross-examination—of which more hereafter.

ILLUSTRATION OF SIMPLE CASE.

Let me illustrate by means of a simple case, in which your Client sues for the price of certain

Ostriches on a verbal sale, delivery to be made, say, a month after the sale, and in which the sale is denied by the Defendant.

THE WISDOM OF GOING ON CIRCUIT.

If the Junior is wise he will go on Circuit to all the Towns, whether he can look forward to any work there or not, and whether the Circuit results in a loss or not. If a loss, it must be regarded as an investment of Capital. By doing so he will become acquainted with the habits of those living in the various Districts, their pursuits and characteristics. He will thus obtain some knowledge of the great industries of the Country, and the needs thereof.

WHAT HE WILL HAVE LEARNT BY SO DOING.

He will have learnt that for successful Ostrich farming, a due amount of Lucerne land and a proper supply of water are required: and that the market for Ostrich feathers fluctuates.

Now assuming that the Plaintiff's version is correct, *What are the possible factors in influencing the Defendant to repudiate the sale?*

The Market for feathers may be down: a fact which of course may cut both ways. Here it becomes necessary to enquire into the ages of the birds sold, and what the growth of the feathers was at the time of sale: for if the birds had been plucked just before the sale, the newly grown feathers would not be fit for Market in a month's time. So that the drop in the Market in such case would not be a sufficient factor in explaining the Defendant's repudiation.

Ostriches require suitable land for running on and Lucerne for feeding. They cannot be run in too large numbers on a given piece of land. Now it may be assumed that when Defendant bought the birds he either had sufficient land and lucerne feeding or had made some provision for obtaining both. If then either of these factors is relevant to the repudiation by the Defendant, it must be because either the Defendant had lost the use of some of his land, or had failed to obtain the land he had made provision for. Enquiry should therefore be directed to these points.

Then, further, *the Defendant might not have been in a position on the day of delivery to pay the price.* Again, it may be assumed, unless he was a mere speculator, that he was able to pay when the contract was made, or expécted that he would be able to pay at the date of delivery. Something must therefore have happened between the dates of sale and delivery to alter the financial position of the Defendant so that he became unable to pay. It is not difficult in most of the Countryside law suits to gather some of the necessary information: on the contrary the difficulty is to separate the Chaff from the Wheat. Enquiry should certainly elicit sufficient facts, if such a change in the Defendant's financial condition has taken place; and it is sometimes found in a direction not easily anticipated. Thus the reason for the repudiation of such a sale was once ascertained to be that the Defendant was a Legatee of considerable property under a will of a Testator domiciled in the Free State: but in the interval between the dates of the sale and of payment, the will had been set aside in the Free State, and the Defendant instead of being well able to pay the price out of the legacy, was not only deprived of this property but was saddled with the payment of moneys raised on the expectant legacy.

Or, again, *the backing of Promissory Notes discounted*, a common method of raising the financial wind, may be the cause of the pecuniary tightness, owing to the insolvency of the maker of the note.

THE ADVANTAGE OF SUCH A COURSE FOR CROSS-EXAMINATION.

By thus directing attention to the various points on which enquiry should be made, Counsel is really collecting a body of instructions which should have been supplied to him, but seldom if ever is: instructions which will also be invaluable to him when he comes to deal with the Defendant in cross-examination, and will prevent his floundering about and asking a number of unnecessary and often dangerous questions. See p. 117 et seq.

The example taken should illustrate what it is suggested that the Junior should do in advising on evidence. It may be objected that this is requiring the Junior to do what should be done by the Attorney. To a certain extent that is the case. But these remarks are intended as a practical guide and not a theoretical treatise, and if the Junior is going to wait for the instructions to contain such information he may wait until the Greek Kalends.

THE ONLY OPPORTUNITY OFTEN OF DIRECTING THE NECESSARY ENQUIRIES.

The objection is only to a certain extent correct. For as he will in all probability not receive his completed Brief until a day or two before the trial, it will be quite impossible, especially in Country cases, to obtain this information so essential for any sort of intelligent cross-examination. The time and the only time when, practically speaking, he can direct his Attorney as to what enquiries should be made is when advising on evidence: for the local Attorney generally comes to Town with the witnesses, and cannot therefore pursue the enquiries even if there were time to do so.

CHAPTER VII.

WHAT WITNESSES SHOULD BE CALLED.

———

In deciding what witnesses he will call from among *those whose statements have been briefed to him,* Counsel will be met at the threshold with this difficulty.

CONFLICT OF INTERESTS ARISING FROM CONSIDERATION OF COSTS.

His Attorney will be anxious that all the witnesses he has subpoenaed should be put into the witness-box; because on taxation of costs the witness expenses of only the necessary witnesses are allowed, and the most natural test of such necessity is the fact that they were actually called. If they are not so called the Attorney meets with trouble on taxation, and if the expenses are not allowed he has to face his Client, who, having won his case, is naturally loath to pay costs out of his own pocket. Sometimes, where a witness is not called, the Taxing Officer will take the Certificate of Counsel that he was a necessary witness: at least I have been asked on occasions to sign such a certificate, and there would be no meaning in doing so except to satisfy the Taxing Officer. But I am dealing with the ordinary and not the exceptional case.

THE RESPONSIBILITY AND BLAME ATTACH TO COUNSEL.

It is obvious that in this case the state of mind of the Attorney will be different from that of Counsel. The former is concerned as to the costs of Taxation: the responsibility of the latter is how best to conduct the case so as to obtain a verdict. And upon one matter Counsel may set his mind at rest: whether he follows the wishes of his Attorney or exercises his own discretion, the responsibility is his: and if he loses the case the blame will be thrown on him, and on him alone. In his own consciousness he may be assured that the blame does not lie solely at his door, especially if he be a Junior and therefore more amenable to pressure from his Attorney and Client: but let him rest perfectly assured that that view will not be shared by his Attorney, and will certainly not be conveyed to his Client. Being thus, colloquially speaking, between the Devil and the Deep Sea, there is no choice for him but to follow his own Judgment.

CONSULTING ATTORNEY.

Not that it is not often of the greatest assistance to consider the views of his Attorney, by no manner of means, especially if he is a man of experience and acumen; but in doing so it is always well to remember that he is looking through what one may call the "taxing glasses," which may cause legal astigmatism.

CONFERENCE WITH WITNESSES.

In deciding in his own judgment whom to call, it will be of the very greatest assistance if Counsel can have a thorough conference with the witnesses. Though called a "conference," it mostly resolves itself into taking the witness over his statement as briefed. In doing so it must cause no surprise, especially in country cases, if the statement of the witness differs in material respects from the briefed proofs, or if the latter require to be modified, amended and supplemented. But it may become necessary to reject some proofs altogether.

WITNESSES AGAINST WHOM TO BE ON GUARD.

There are three classes of witnesses from the Country against whom it is well to be on guard.

(1)   THE CAPE TOWN TRIPPER.

The first of them is the witness who sees the opportunity of obtaining a cheap trip to Cape Town and succumbing to the fascinations of the Capital at the expense of the litigant. He knows something about the facts in dispute, but not enough to justify bringing him down at great expense: and therefore to ensure his obtaining his Cape Town trip, his statements *as briefed* in situ will be most emphatic, unqualified and convincing. He is generally late at the conference or is not to be found at all: and when he does present himself or is discovered after much searching has the appearance of having had a " great night out," the signs of a debauch, which he will endeavour to carry off by the " cock-sure " effrontery which has enabled him to come to Town. But it is mere camouflage, and judicious questioning will enable Counsel to judge that he will never stand cross-examination for many minutes. But these gentlemen are full of high spirits, bonhomie and assurance, and are very popular with the Client, who thinks a great deal of their evidence. He will constantly interrupt other witnesses and try to put them " right "—as he says—and if allowed will take control of the whole proceedings, his object being to impress everyone with his knowledge and cleverness and interest in the case. But it is all camouflage. I have described him as well as I can, so that by these " finger-prints " may he be known and guarded against, for he is quite a well-defined type.

(2) THE WITNESS WHO ATTENDS CONFERENCES ON BOTH SIDES.

The next class of witness to be careful of is the gentleman who is so friendly with both sides that he is briefed on both sides and attends conferences on both sides, though he may be subpoenaed only on your Client's side. At the preliminary stages of the conference I have found it best to call in one witness at a time, and not to have a whole number in together, as is so often the practice. In a crowd of witnesses such a gentleman may escape detection or much mischief may be done before he is discovered. Where each witness is called in separately it is easier to find out if he has been attending or is about to attend a conference on the other side.

When Counsel has decided that a Witness falls under either of the aforementioned classes, and is not to be called, he should keep this decision to himself and the Counsel briefed with him—for obvious reasons. The Witness of the lastmentioned class should of course not be requested to attend any further conferences.

HOW TO DEAL WITH A WITNESS SUBPOENAED ON BOTH SIDES.

It will sometimes be ascertained,—every effort should be made to obtain the information—before going into Court that a Witness has been subpoenaed on both sides—which may also account for his *legitimately* attending the conferences on both sides. If he is a mere formal witness this is immaterial: if he is more than that, the position requires some consideration. You will in such case, of course, ask him if he has given a statement to the other side, for it does not follow that because he has been subpoenaed by your opponent therefore a statement has been taken from him.

SUBPOENAING A WITNESS WHO IS NOT INTENDED TO BE CALLED.

A witness is sometimes subpoenaed without the least intention of calling him: the real object being to assure his attendance in Court. For he may be a witness whom your opponent ought in the circumstances of the case to call. But he may be a dangerous or undesirable witness for the other side, or he may be considered to be such, and therefore when his undesirability is ascertained he is either left at home by the opponent or he is sent back home by the first train. To make sure therefore that this shall not take place the witness is subpoenaed by your side as well. Attention is then drawn to him in the examination of the opposing witnesses, generally of the opponent himself, and the latter is asked whether the witness is in Court, the object of course being to make the Court or Jury mindful that the witness is present and therefore available for being called. If your opponent does not call him, you draw attention in your address to the fact that he is present and available and nevertheless has not been called.

This subpoenaing of a witness whom there is no intention of calling, is sometimes done even when your opponent has not subpoenaed him at all: and for the same reasons.

SUCH WITNESS MAY NOT HAVE GIVEN A STATEMENT TO THE OTHER SIDE.

It does not follow therefore that where your witness has been subpoenaed by your opponent he has given a statement to the other side. But he may have done so, in which case it is of course more dangerous to call him than if he has not done so.

WHERE WITNESS HAS GIVEN SUCH A STATEMENT.

If he admits that he has done so, I never found it of any use to ask him what such statement contained. It is not likely that he will admit that he has given your Attorney one version and that he has given your opponent another version. Such a witness generally asserts that the version given to your opponent is the same as that which he is giving you. This may be so or it may not.

A. SOME PRACTICAL SUGGESTIONS WHERE WITNESS IS RELIABLE AND INTELLIGENT.

If the witness is a man of intelligence and standing and not the kind of person who will make and sign any sort of statement which the particular side interviewing him desires, then, allowing for the human failing of forgetfulness, etc., it may be assumed that the statements given to both sides are the same. Then comes the question why, if this is so, was he subpoenaed by the other side? because ex hypothesi his statement is in favour of your side.

1. It will generally be found in such cases that the evidence of the witness is *not wholly in your favour*: that some one or other portion thereof supports your opponent's side. That throws on you the necessity of considering whether the parts favourable to your opponent are so important as to outweigh or equalize the importance of the parts in your favour.

If they are, do not call him. And, indeed, if you can do without his evidence, so much the better.

2. But suppose his evidence *is wholly in your favour*, what reason actuates your opponent in calling him? It may be that this has been done for the very purpose of inducing you not to call him: but it may also be that there is something which the witness is keeping back or has forgotten or deemed of no importance which has in fact *an important* bearing on the case. One never knows quite what to expect and to ask for: it depends on the circumstances of the case, and very much on your foresight and acumen in putting questions to him in conference, so as to make him recall the past.

The sort of danger here indicated may perhaps best be understood by an illustration.

Suppose the dispute is one as to the boundaries of a farm, and the witness is called to depose to the fact that as far as his knowledge went your Client always grazed his cattle over the disputed area. You call him and in cross-examination he admits that some twenty years ago he entered into an agreement with the opponent's predecessor in title to cut reeds on this very disputed ground. Now what are you to do if this is sprung on you in Court? If you ask him in re-examination what were the circumstances which led him to make the arrangement you may obtain an explanation which does away with the prima facie effect of his evidence, or you may get something in reply still more damaging. It is clear that you cannot leave the evidence as it stands and therefore you must risk the reply.

The *proper time therefore to try and ascertain if the witness is keeping something back, etc., is of course at the conference.* He should then have been asked and pressed whether he had ever done or said anything from which it might be inferred that he

recognized the title of your opponent to the land:
and it may then have been found that the witness was
under the impression that the opponent's predecessor had a *servitude* over the disputed land which required that the consent to the reeds being cut should
be given. The exercise of such a supposed servitude
may corroborate the user of the land by your Client
for the purpose of *grazing*, which is really all that
the witness had any *knowledge of*. In any case, whatever the explanation, you will be warned beforehand
and can judge whether you will call him or not

B. WHERE WITNESS IS NOT SUCH A RELIABLE AND IN-
TELLIGENT ONE.

But if the witness be of a different stamp from that
stated under heading A, so that you cannot feel assured that the version he gave your opponent is the
same as that given you, then do not call him. If you
do, do not be surprised if he is cross-examined on a
version which is damaging to your side.

FURTHER HINTS ON " CONFERENCES."

ACQUIRING MATERIAL FOR CROSS-EXAMINATION.

Before leaving the subject of " Conferences," it
may not be out of place here to make the Junior
mindful of the following precautionary measures.
As I have pointed out to him, he will seldom receive
any instructions upon which he can base any cross-
examination of the opposite party. But the latter's
witnesses have *also* to be cross-examined, and it
would certainly be most exceptional to find any material briefed for dealing with them.

But it seldom happens that your Attorney, or your
Client or his witnesses are all ignorant of the persons to be called by your opponent. In the case of
witnesses coming from the Country, they generally

all, on both sides, leave by the same train. So that upon enquiry at the conference you can obtain a fairly complete list of, at any rate, the persons subpoenaed for the opposite side. Then question your Attorney and your witnesses at the conference as to anything they may know about the past and present character, the bias, or prejudice or interests, etc., of the witnesses on his list, and note the information.

It is obvious that the party who obtains the information who the witnesses are that have been subpoenaed for his opponent, should have a great advantage. Because it enables enquiry to be made as to their motives, interest, prejudice, etc.: all information of the very greatest use in dealing with them in cross-examination. And it is also obvious that the earlier in the litigation proceedings this information is obtained, the greater the advantage. Now it sometimes surprises the Junior that in some cases the names of the opponent's witnesses are accurately known: in others, there is no such or very little information. The reason for this difference very often lies in the fact that in the former cases the Country Attorney is the Deputy Sheriff: in the latter he is not.

Now I do not wish to be misunderstood when I suggest that this is not a proper state of affairs. The Deputy Sheriffs in the Western Province—and I have no doubt that the same applies elsewhere—are men of the highest standing in their profession—indeed, if they were not, they would not be selected and appointed as Deputy Sheriffs, and no one would be more justifiably indignant at the merest suggestion that they would think of taking advantage of their position as Deputies. But the fact remains that they are the persons who can serve the subpoenaes upon witnesses, and therefore they cannot help becoming acquainted with the names of the witnesses called in a Civil suit. If then a Deputy happens to be the Country Attorney in such a suit he becomes acquainted with all the names of the witnesses opposed to him, and can therefore give the information to Counsel when required. Where such Deputy is himself the practitioner appearing in the local Magistrate's Court, he has the same advantage of knowing who will be called against him. This should not be. High as is the character of Deputies, *no Deputy being the Attorney on either side* should be placed in such a position, for reasons which must be obvious.

For the same reasons, where witnesses are requested to be subpoenaed for his defence by an Accused person, the subpoenaes should not be served by the particular members of the Police Force who are concerned for the prosecution. Being human, they are interested that those, whom they consider to be guilty persons, should be brought to justice: and therefore they should not be placed in the position of coming into contact with the witnesses for the defence, no matter how high their character as Police may be.

ADMISSIONS, CHARACTER, ETC.

The Conference is also the proper occasion on which to obtain from your witnesses the explanations of any admissions made in documentary evidence or verbally to any person: and to enquire into any matters affecting the character of your witnesses.

WITNESSES TO BE GUARDED AGAINST
(*Continued*).

3. THE LOCAL EXPERT.

Another class is that of the local expert who is very much in evidence in such matters as disputes about water-rights. He is generally a man of good standing in the District, and of means, and of influence. Apparently, he may have no interest in the case; but this is a matter which must be enquired into.

The nature of the enquiry in the case of your own witnesses will also be a guide as to dealing with the local experts called for your opponent. Now in such a matter, for example, as a water dispute, the point of view of the upper and the lower proprietors on a stream naturally differs very much. If your Client is an upper proprietor, his expert witnesses will confessedly be men who regard the issues involved from the point of view of upper proprietors, and vice versa. And although they are not interested in the particular *dispute* before the Court, they may be most vitally —in a greater or lesser degree—interested in the *principles* involved in the dispute. Now the more impartial your witness is, the more weight should his evidence have. And it sometimes happens that among the experts on your side will be found a *lower proprietor*. This on the face of it should make him a valuable witness, for his evidence and his apparent interests are opposed. But things are not always what they seem. Although a lower proprietor, it may be found that the farm which he inhabits and personally works is well provided with, and safeguarded by servitudes and agreements as to water, but that he has interests in other localities in land which is on the upper parts of some other stream, and that as a fact he is greatly interested in the success of your Client's case. It must be remembered that the affairs and land interests of leading farmers are well known in the Country Districts, and that your opponents may be well aware of the real interest of the witness in the success of your Client. I think that it is better to produce a witness confessedly an upper Proprietor than to produce one, whose apparent interests lie with the lower proprietors, and whose real interests are shown on cross-examination to be those of a lower proprietor.

WHOM TO CALL AFTER ELIMINATION OF " DANGEROUS " WITNESSES.

Having by means of the conference eliminated such witnesses as you conclude it is too dangerous to call, the next question to decide is who of those that remain you will call. The only advice I think that can be of practical assistance is this: make for quality rather than for numbers in your witnesses.

DANGER OF NUMBERS.

It must always be borne in mind that every additional witness on the same issue is exposing your case to the further danger of cross-examination. Do not be influenced merely by the fact that the witnesses have been subpoenaed, or that the Attorney or the Client desires them to be called. Cases have been known to be lost through calling the very last witness on an issue, because it has been urged on the Junior that he " must call that man: he is an excellent witness." And remember, as has been pointed out, the blame will settle on you should you lose the case, whether you call the witness or not.

" PILING " UP WITNESSES.

It is becoming more and more the practice to " pile up " the witnesses, to use a colloquial expression, all deposing to the same state of facts. What impression this makes may be well illustrated by a remark I have heard more than once fall from the late Chief Justice, and spoken in a tone of weary irritation that was only too eloquent: " Oh! Mr. —— ask him if he agrees with the last witness, and then leave it to cross-examination."

CHAPTER VIII.

THE ORDER OF EXAMINING THE WITNESSES.

———

THE FIRST Rule is that *they should be examined in order of sequence of events* so that the story runs connectedly and intelligibly. But it often happens that there are more than one witness who speak to the same facts; or that the sequence of events is not the most important element, e.g., in disputes as to boundaries of land, use of water, and the like. The question then arises, in what order to call your witnesses. The latter will of course differ in intelligence, in character, standing, and capability of undergoing cross-examination. Upon the intelligence and standing one may be able to rely: upon the point of standing cross-examination I do not think anyone can be certain. I have gone into Court feeling certain that my Client must lose, and the witnesses have stood the ordeal so unexpectedly and remarkably well, that the case was won: I have on the other hand been convinced that nothing would shake some witnesses and they have made a most pitiable exhibition. Opinions moreover differ as to the best course to pursue: whether the best and strongest witnesses should be produced one after the other in order to produce the first and most favourable impression: or whether, as I have heard suggested, there should be a sort of alternation of first a strong, and then a weak, and then again a strong witness: or whether some strong evi-

dence should be kept for the last. Some practitioners
think that if all the strong witnesses are called first,
and the evidence tails off to a number of weak witnesses, easily broken down in cross-examination, the
effect of the strong evidence, especially in a case
which lasts days, is greatly lost. Others believe in
getting in their hard and strong blows first. There
seems force in both opinions: but I do not doubt that
if a strong witness of repute, especially if he is *not a*
party to the suit, can be kept until near the end of
a long case, his evidence comes with greater force and
effect than if it were merely " piled up " at the beginning after other strong evidence. This does not mean,
however, that you must begin with your weak evidence and leave your best and strongest until the
end. It means that you should get in hard and strong
blows from the first, but *not all* your blows so that
you are exhausted. Keep a reserve of strength, if you
can, for the knock-out. In this respect a battle in
the forensic arena is like any other fight.

CHAPTER IX.

EXAMINATION IN CHIEF.

MY EXPERIENCE in my Junior days was that whenever I sought advice and counsel from such books as were available, I arose from a study of such advice with the firm conviction that I must inevitably, in examining my witnesses, commit blunder after blunder and make a consummate ass of myself. As the work of Counsel is done openly, coram populo, it is not possible to hide or bury one's blunders. Moreover a beginner is naturally nervous: so that the " advice " or " hints " did not do much to restore any self-confidence. They consisted mainly of a great number of " don'ts," which no doubt conveyed a great deal to the experienced man, but left me in a more hopeless fog than before, and while the poor brain was in a state of ghastly confusion in trying to avoid all the dangers it was warned against, there was precious little " advice " or " counsel " as to what the Junior was to *do* as a set off against the very many things which he was *not* to do. Whether or not any advice of mine will be of any more practical value may be doubted: nevertheless one can but try to give the practitioner some idea of what it is wise to do, as well as to warn him against what he should not do.

THE PRINCIPAL RULE IS, PUT YOUR BRIEF IN ORDER.

This may appear somewhat strange advice stated in this bald way: but I hope that its true meaning will become apparent as the practitioner reads on.

The best way to deal with any feeling of nervousness is to try and master the brief: but in dealing with a trial case in which witnesses have to be examined, the brief will not be mastered properly unless the statements of the witnesses are drawn up in chronological and proper sequence of order, with all the necessary corroborations, explanations and conversations in their proper places. It may be said that this is surely what Counsel may expect when the brief on trial is delivered: no doubt that is so theoretically: in practice it is very often only an expectation. The reason is not far to seek.

Briefed Statements Often Require Emendation, etc.

It often happens that after the original statement has been taken, additions must be made on various points, as they emerge into prominence upon the statements of other witnesses being taken: and in the conference with witnesses Counsel will have made erasures, amendments and additional notes. All this evidence must be brought into due and proper chronological and sequence of order.

Want of Natural Sequence Must Be Avoided.

Nothing is worse than to finish the main line of examination and then to expect the witness to hark back to different points and to add thereto and elaborate or explain them according to the order in which Counsel has them in *his* brief—if not put in proper order. It is easy enough for Counsel to deal with them because he has them in writing before him: but the witness is in quite a different position. He has to rely on his memory: and to expect him to jump from one incident to another in no order of sequence, without getting confused and without forgetting important matters, is to expect the impossible.

ALL ADDITIONS, ETC., MUST BE NOTED IN THEIR PROPER
ORDER OF TIME.

All the additions, alterations, explanations should
be in their proper and natural place if the evidence
is to have its due and proper weight. This is sometimes no light matter when the brief is only delivered
shortly before the trial and the witnesses' statements
are long and numerous: but it has to be done, no
matter though you see the break of dawn while still
at work on the statements. I have on various occasions rewritten in brief the whole of the statements
of the principal witnesses: and I remember one case
in which the brief was delivered on Saturday for trial
on the following Monday. It was *a most complicated
question as to the right of discharge of water* by
various ditches and water-courses: the statements of
the witnesses were very sketchy, but the worst feature
was that they did not follow any kind of sequence,
*but had been taken down as the witnesses remem-
bered this or that incident,* or as their interlocutor
noted one or other of the points in issue. It was impossible to examine upon the statements: so my
Junior and I went out to the situs on the intermedi-
ate Sunday, and spent the greater part of the day in
taking the statements ourselves. This gave us a great
pull over our opponents, who were very little better
off in their briefs than we had been. Yes: we pulled
it off.

The statements of the witnesses therefore should
follow in proper chronological order and in sequence
of events. *All conversations to be given must be in
their due place.*

If any explanation is required from the witness
either of his own evidence or of some statement which
will be made by some other witness, it must be noted
at the place where it properly fits in. All documentary evidence must be carefully marked in the state-

ment in due order. If this is done thoroughly and properly then the Junior may feel assured that he will avoid some of the greatest blunders which are so apt to be committed in examination in chief.

WHAT BLUNDERS ARE THUS AVOIDED.

I. *He will avoid confusing his witness* by making him jump in mental exercise from one order of time to another, a very difficult thing for him when he is probably more nervous even than Counsel. His story should run on in the natural order as he will remember it. How often does one not hear a practitioner say to a witness: "Oh! I forgot to ask you whether, etc.," harking back to something to which the witness deposed, it may be some quarter of an hour or more ago, with the result that the witness has forgotten all about it: and worse still cannot easily take up the thread of his story again where he was interrupted.

II. *The practitioner will not overlook any part of the evidence* necessary to be deposed to. But when the statement of the witness is written out with the amendments, explanations, etc., occurring as they *emerged on taking the statements,* nothing is easier than either to overlook some of the evidence, or to examine the witness again upon what he has already deposed to—with dire results.

(a) MATERIAL FACTS SHOULD BE ELICITED IN CHIEF.

The practitioner should strive to bring out all the relevant and material facts in examination in chief; should he overlook any, and the facts be elicited on cross-examination, a very bad impression may be created. Very often one hears the Judge comment on the fact, that the answer was only elicited in cross-examination, in a manner which leaves no doubt as to what he thinks of it: and the opposite side will make much of such facts in argument to his advantage.

The reason for this is very natural. It is to be expected that a witness called for your Client will have stated everything that he can in the latter's favour. If, therefore, he omits something that is material and only deposes to it when asked on cross-examination, the question at once suggests itself: why did he not tell this to his own side? It creates the impression that the answer may be either an afterthought or not a truthful one: in any case it loses the value it would have if it had been deposed to in examination-in-Chief.

(*b*) MATERIAL EVIDENCE SOMETIMES PURPOSELY OMITTED.

There is no doubt that sometimes some matter is purposely omitted in examination-in-Chief as a "trap" for the opposing side to fall into. But I would not advise a young practitioner to do so. It requires a great deal of experience before one can judge properly whether it is a wise thing to set this "trap." The opposing Counsel, moreover, may see the snare prepared for him and avoid it, with the result that the evidence on the point is not elicited, unless there is another witness who can supply the omission. It is better, I think, for the practitioner to lay all his evidence before the Court.

III. WHAT BLUNDERS AVOIDED (*continued*).

Counsel will avoid interrupting his witness in the course of an answer.

This is a blunder which should be carefully guarded against. Always let the witness finish what he is saying before you interrupt him for some explanation. You may be able to pick up the thread again, but it is not an easy matter for the witness after such an explanation to comply with the bland request, "now go on with what you were saying." How can he possibly remember?

At any rate if you do make this faux pas, assist him by reminding him of what he was saying when you interrupted him. Let us hope that you at least will remember it. But do not expect him to continue without such assistance.

For these reasons I cannot urge too strongly upon the young practitioner to get all his proofs, and statements of witnesses in chronological order and due sequence, even if he has to rewrite them and arrange them as they should be. Moreover he will find that this will give him considerable confidence, knowing that he has thought and mapped out everything of importance: that he has in short mastered his brief.

CRIMINAL PROSECUTIONS.

These suggestions apply to criminal prosecutions as well as to Civil actions. Most young Counsel are given the opportunity of prosecuting; their brief consisting of the depositions taken at the Preparatory Examination. Such depositions cannot be expected to be in the same chronological order and sequence as the statements of the witnesses in Civil suits *should* be. For the deposition as deposed to must be signed by the witness and cannot be re-arranged and put into shape by the Magistrate before it is signed. Whereas an Attorney before briefing is in a position to do so in a Civil Suit. It follows therefore that depositions cannot and do not state all the facts in due order of sequence. But if the evidence of the Crown witnesses is to be clear, comprehensible and complete, such deposition must necessarily be re-arranged. Merely underscoring the relevant statements is of little avail in that direction: it only means often that the deposition is blue-pencilled.

Years ago it was the common practice to give the Junior a copy of the depositions, if he asked for it, on his leaving Cape Town for Circuit. This enabled him to put some order into the Brief. Nowadays I am given to understand that the Junior does not get the depositions until he arrives in the Circuit Town —it may be the afternoon before the Court opens. If this is so, then it is not a system conducive to efficient prosecution without undue waste of time. For the examination even of a Crown witness means something more than the underscoring with a blue pencil. This may be enough for the experienced practitioner: it most certainly is not for the young practitioner, who might very usefully follow and adopt the suggestions I have ventured to make as to putting *the brief in order.*

EXAMINING FROM THE BRIEF.

In examining a witness in chief I have heard or read it stated that Counsel should not examine from his brief. I do not follow this advice in the case of a beginner. It may be very good counsel for the experienced and collected practitioner: but in the case of the nervous beginner who is as apt as—if not more so than—the witness to forget matters of importance, it seems to me safer to follow the brief.

KEEP YOUR TEMPER.

The next and most important rule is, "*Keep your temper.*" This should apply to the whole conduct of a case, not merely to the examination in Chief. There is nothing more depressing than to see Counsel with long and serious faces when matters appear to be becoming critical. Their state of mind is soon communicated to the Attorneys: and whatever the psychological cause may be, the Client and the principal witnesses become affected also: and this atmosphere reacts upon their evidence.

But worst of all, the temper of everyone concerned on your client's side is also affected: and there is a tendency for Counsel to become irritable and short-tempered with his *own witnesses*, as if it were their fault that matters appear to be going wrong. In cases before a Jury this state of mind will be of great advantage to your opponents.

Baiting a Bad-Tempered Counsel.

Juries delight in the battle of wits between Counsel; and nothing pleases them more, judging from their smiles and chuckles, than to have a Counsel " drawn ", to see the " galled jade wince." So it is part of the tactics of some Advocates to bait the opposing Counsel in order to make him lose his temper: and when he becomes irritable and bad tempered, nothing is easier than to raise the laugh against him. But it is bad Advocacy to have the Jury amused at your expense. Keep your temper and a smiling imperturbable countenance, and you are in a better position to return the compliment. Laugh *with* the Jury, if it must be so: it takes away much of the sting.

But far worse than all this is to lose your temper *with your own witness*. When one has a stupid or dull one to deal with, it is sometimes a great strain to control one's feelings and not to show annoyance. Such a witness irritates everyone. Your Junior, if you have one, will probably begin to think that he could deal with the witness far better than you can, and will become pressing with his questions and suggestions, even to pulling your gown to attract your

attention : your Attorney will most likely be of the
same opinion; with the result that you will have one
person pouring advice into one ear, and another
whispering his counsel into the other ear; your opponents are audibly rejoicing and chuckling; while a
cutting remark from the Bench on the value of the
testimony may add to your general sense of well-
being (!). If under these circumstances you lose
your temper and glare at the unfortunate witness,
and repeat the question in a louder tone of voice—
all of which you most certainly must not do—then
you are throwing your Client's case away. Restrain
your temper, and if you have learnt to smile as the
Boxer smiles when he gets a " facer," then smile:
waive your two would-be advisers politely (or otherwise) to their seats, disregard this multiplicity of
counsel—for you are more likely to find confusion
than wisdom in it—and with patience and quietness
follow the course you had mapped out for yourself.

But if you begin to give heed to and listen to first
the one and then the other you will soon find yourself—and your witness—in a hopeless fog.

WHERE WITNESS GIVES THE OPPOSITE ANSWER TO THE
ONE EXPECTED.

It sometimes happens, through various causes, that
the witness will give the very opposite answer to the
one which his statement leads you to expect. This
is sure to elicit smiles and pronounced glee from your
opponents: and the Judge may be inwardly—and out-
wardly—much amused: but keep your temper and a
bland face. I knew a Counsel who, when he received
a facer of this kind, would respond with an imperturbable face, " Quite so, quite so," as if it did not
really matter. If it did not serve to completely break
the force of the blow, it at any rate puzzled the Jury,
as I have often noted. They could not understand

why the opposing Advocates were making such demonstrations of delight, when the witness's Counsel seemed not only unmoved by the answer, but to acquiesce in it.

WHAT TO DO.

What then is the best thing to do under these circumstances? It may be assumed that the statement in the brief is correct, and therefore that the answer is the result of some mistake, misapprehension, or confusion. It may have been caused by some interruption for which you have or have not been responsible: it may have been the result of your expecting the witness to perform mental athletics by jumping from one period of time to another out of the proper sequence. If so, the best course is to go back a little in the witness' statement and to go over a little of the sequence of events leading up to the stage when he gave the unexpected answer. This will probably do away with the confusion, etc., which existed when the first answer was given, and then when he has corrected himself, he can be got to explain that his first answer was under a misapprehension or mistake.

DON'T BLAME THE WITNESS.

But do not when you get the first answer either get irritable or annoyed with the witness, and do not repeat the question in a louder tone as if he were deaf. That will not help him, and will probably only accentuate his confusion and mistake.

If he repeats the error and the answer is not of importance leave it alone: the probability is that your opponent not observing the advice, hereafter to be tendered, of " leaving well alone," will, when he comes to cross-examine, press your witness upon this answer, with the result that the mistake will be made manifest to him, and he will correct his answer and explain that it was a mistake. In that correction you can further assist him in re-examination.

WHERE ANSWER OF IMPORTANCE: WHAT DO NOT DO.

If the matter is of importance, leave the answer alone for a time. Do not go on repeating it, which is really the cross-examination of your own witness, and will be sure to call up your opponent on to his feet with the objection to the Bench that you are cross-examining your own witness. The result will be that the Judge will admonish and stop you, and it may become impossible to repair the mistake.

BUT WHAT DO.

What I would counsel is to leave the answer alone for a time, until you have brought your witness to testify to some fact which shows that the answer under consideration could not have been correct. You can then put the original question again, and the witness' mind being cleared he will correct himself, and then you can draw attention to his original answer and get the explanation as to its being a mistake.

The next general rule—which indeed applies to cross-examination as well—is *LEAVE WELL ALONE.*

When your witness has given the answer which his statement leads you to expect, leave it alone. Junior practitioners—and not only Juniors at that—are so prone to emphasize the point made in answer by repeating it with such remarks as " Are you sure," " Are you quite certain."

The idea of Counsel is either to impress the Judge or Jury with the importance of the fact or to guard against their not paying attention to it. If the matter is of such importance as to justify emphasizing, be assured that the Judge, who is much more experienced than you are, has fully appreciated the value of the testimony. Repetition may only bring upon you—as it has on me—the admonishment, sometimes in no uncertain tone, that " the witness has already answered that question three or four times."

With some Jurors the repetition by way of " are you quite certain " is apt to leave the impression that neither you nor the witness was sure of it.

Once you have the answer, it is recorded, and if it is of any importance, you can emphasize it for all you are worth when addressing the Jury. If by chance the value of it should have been *overlooked*—which is not very probable unless you have rushed the evidence of the witness—I do not think that you will prejudice your case by your calling attention to it only in your address. Quite apart from the consideration that there will be several points in your case, the bearing of which may not be very apparent to the Jury until you point them out—and you cannot very well emphasize every point in the evidence— there is this to be noted. How often in daily life do we not find this experience. A man is advancing a certain view based upon certain facts and information and you thereupon point out to him some fact which has escaped his attention. Note the tone of his voice in which he ejaculates, as the force of this factor breaks upon his view, " —— I quite overlooked that." Of course, consideration may show him that the factor is after all not of such great importance: but that does not militate against the view, that calling attention to the evidence in your address is quite as effective as—if not more so—getting the witness to repeat his answer.

DANGERS OF REPEATING A QUESTION.

So much for the advantages, if any: but now consider the dangers of the repetition.

(*a*)   DOUBT IN WITNESS' MIND.

There is the danger of the witness beginning to have a doubt himself, because the question suggests a doubt. Sometimes, when a question is repeated, the witness has the most transparent expression on his face of asking himself—" Have I given the wrong answer?"

(*b*)   ANSWER IN DIFFERENT TERMS.

There is the danger of his not giving the answer in the same terms as before; and

(*c*)   HE MAY GIVE REASONS WHY.

And there is the greatest danger of all, of his being too ready to assist you in emphasizing the certainty in his mind by referring to the *reasons why* he is so certain.

HEARSAY AND EXAGGERATION.

He may introduce some hearsay evidence, e.g., what somebody else who saw the incident said. To most people the fact that another person, present when the incident took place, took the same view of the facts as he did, is corroborative. What they do not appreciate is that a witness who is sure and certain of his facts does not generally rely on what such other person says. In short it argues *some doubt*, it may be a little, but nevertheless some, in his own mind, which he is relieved to find is dissipated by the other eye-witness taking the same view of the facts as he does. The witness, therefore, by introducing such hearsay evidence, which the Examiner did not want to elicit, but which he in fact does elicit by the repetition of his question, creates some atmosphere of doubt instead of making assurance doubly sure.

Or he may exaggerate some fact which emphasizes why he is so certain: all of which reasons simply afford excellent material for cross-examination.

REFERENCE TO SOME OTHER EVENT.

Thus he may give as his reason the fact that some other event happened at the same time. This may sound plausible. But if the events are of equal importance, why should he remember the last mentioned event any better than the one he is testifying to? Moreover, he can now be cross-examined as to the correctness of his memory with regard to such last-mentioned event. Thus your opponent has a double attack. Should the witness be shaken upon the accuracy of his memory upon the reason adduced by him his evidence upon the fact in issue becomes of little value.

EAGERNESS TO EMPHASIZE.

Moreover a witness is sometimes quite as eager to emphasize a point, the importance of which is apparent to him, as the practitioner is. Although his statement of fact may be perfectly correct and truthful, it is human nature to try and make assurance doubly sure. Such a witness should be restrained rather than encouraged in his corroboration, unless the latter has been carefully gone into.

Thus a witness may in corroboration of his verbal statement refer to or produce some writing or notebook.

REFERENCE TO WRITING—REFRESHING MEMORY. (See pp. 79 and 106).

Such writing or entry (*where they are in themselves not evidence*) if made at the time of or immediately after the event testified to may be used—technically—to *refresh his memory*, though *in effect* they are certainly corroborative evidence. But then few persons know that the entry is only admissible if made as stated, i.e., at the time: so when he becomes aware of this necessity in the witness box, either owing to a genuine confusion of memory or from a desire to support and corrobate the case, the witness will assert that the entry was made at the time.

SUCH NOTES MUST BE CAREFULLY EXAMINED.

It is well therefore before any reference is made to such writings or entries to examine them very carefully and thoroughly *yourself*, both where they are to be produced for your own side, and where your opponents have given notice of avail. In the latter case examine the originals yourself. I remember a case in which an Insurance Company was the defendant in an action brought against it to recover a sum of money for which it was alleged by the Plaintiff that he had insured property since destroyed by fire. Everything turned upon the date of a receipt which bore a cancelled penny stamp, the Defendants denying that the receipt had been given on that date. The Plaintiff gave notice of avail and *the receipt was examined*. At the trial the Defendants were able to produce conclusive evidence to prove that the particular issue of which the cancelled stamp formed one, had not been issued for sale until some weeks *after* the alleged date of Cancellation: whereupon Counsel for Plaintiff withdrew, in Court, from the case.

Notes " left at home."

It constantly happens that these writings or entries "have been left at home" by the witness. They should be immediately sent for before coming into Court, and attention should be carefully directed to the *chronological order* of the entries, *sequence of dates*, the *colour of the ink,* the *kind of paper*, and the *facility for obtaining such paper* by the witness (p. 107).

If doubtful—

In short, such writings or entries should be most carefully looked into. If the documentary corroboration is at all suspicious, eliminate it from your case.

As to cross-examination on such entries, etc., see p. 106 and seq.

Nothing is worse than to allow the impression to be formed that your witness has been trying to bolster up his case by "afterthought."

Leave well alone, and don't try to make well better unless you are sure of your ground. If you are, then certainly corroborate your verbal evidence by the writing or entries the best way allowable.

Examination of your witnesses.

There are some general Rules in the Examination of your witnesses in chief which may be of practical use.

1. *The evidence must not be hearsay*: or to put the rule in a *positive* way, you must produce the *best* evidence available. This is not a treatise on the Law of Evidence, and consequently the advice now given is very general: but it will be found, I trust, to be a good ordinary working basis, especially for the Country practitioner.

The *best evidence* means what it conveys: it is the best proof of the fact which it is desired to establish: and the practitioner should always ask himself to test this rule, " which is the best way of proving the allegation of fact."

If *a document is to be proved*, say *a will*, clearly the best evidence is the will itself. But suppose the will is *lost* and there is a *copy*, then the *copy* can be proved, provided of course it is first proved that the will is lost, otherwise you will be met with the objection that the best evidence is not being produced. If there is *no copy* of the will, then you prove the contents of the will *through witnesses who have read* the original or have heard it read. In such a case it is clear that the original will is better than a copy, if it is available: if not, then a copy is better than the oral testimony of people who have merely read it or heard it read: if there is neither original nor copy, the next best evidence is such oral testimony.

Again, suppose A wants to prove that on B having sent A an offer to sell a horse for £—, A accepted the offer and sent his messenger X to B with a *message* stating that A *accepted the offer*.

Now what is the best evidence? The point A must make is that the acceptance was communicated to B. The best evidence is of course that of X, who deposes to the fact that he told B that the offer was accepted. His is indeed the only actual evidence that the acceptance was communicated to B.

Very elementary! Yes. But over and over again it will be found that practitioners try to prove this acceptance by tendering the evidence of A that he sent X with the message and that X came back *and reported that he had given the message to B, who thereupon said to X, etc.*

In a recent case the Plaintiff wanted to prove that a donkey in the possession of B, not the Defendant, was the plaintiff's property. It appeared that a Judgment Creditor X had taken out a Writ of Execution against B, and the Sheriff's Officer had gone to B's farm and attached the donkey, whereupon B said to the Officer that the donkey was not his property but belonged to the Plaintiff. The Plaintiff called the Officer and produced his evidence that B had said that the donkey belonged to the Plaintiff. Now if B had been the Defendant then of course any admission made by him to another person would have been admissible, but not being a party to the suit any such statement made by B is *res inter alios acta* and is not admissible. The best evidence that the donkey in B's possession belonged to the Plaintiff is clearly that of B himself.

2. LEADING QUESTIONS MUST NOT BE PUT TO WITNESSES.

This is amplified and illustrated on pages 72-4, 81-3.

3. A PARTY CANNOT CROSS-EXAMINE HIS OWN WITNESS,

simply because he gives evidence which is not favourable to him. But there are circumstances when the party may do so: they are dealt with on page 75 under the heading "Hostile Witnesses."

4. A PARTY CANNOT DISCREDIT OR CONTRADICT HIS OWN WITNESS.

Where a witness you have called gives evidence which is not favourable to your side, you cannot there and then proceed to prove that he is not worthy of credence, nor can you proceed *forthwith* to call some other witness, or produce a statement in writing by him, to contradict him. The course which you have to pursue in such a case is dealt with on pages 75-6 under headings "Hostile Witness" and "Inconsistent Statement."

CHAPTER X.

WHAT QUESTIONS MAY BE ASKED.

———

THE MAIN theoretical Rule is that *Leading Questions may not be put.*

A leading question may be described as one which *suggests the answer desired,* or one which *embodies a statement of fact and admits of a definite answer* by way of a simple " Yes " or " No.". This seems to me to be not a definition but a description. Thus it does not seem to me to be absolutely correct to say that it is always a test of a leading question that the answer to it of " Yes " or " No " is conclusive.

For instance, suppose a witness has deposed to a conversation and has forgotten to mention *some material* portion, the question is constantly put and allowed, " Did he say anything about so and so?"

But whether the Examiner would be allowed to call the attention of the witness to a *number* of material portions of the conversation is another matter. There are various occasions when a leading question may be put without objection. Thus where the question is one of identification of a person, the latter may be produced and confronted with the witness, who may then be asked directly, " Is that the man?"

Leading is not an absolute but a relative term, and it is obvious that what might be unobjectionable under certain circumstances may become very leading and objectionable.

ILLUSTRATIONS OF WHAT IS A LEADING QUESTION.

It is not always easy for a beginner to appreciate the application of this rule, so let me illustrate. Suppose the question in issue is whether the Defendant was on a certain date in January in possession of a white ox, the property of the Plaintiff. A witness is called to prove this. After the formal questions of name, etc., the examination proceeds:

Q. *Did you see the Defendant in the month of January last?*

A. *Yes.*

Theoretically this is a leading question, because it embodies the material fact that witness saw the Defendant in January, and admits of the conclusive answer in the affirmative. But it would take so long to bring the witness to the point when and where he met the Defendant on the particular occasion in issue that such a question is not disallowed, unless *the* point is whether the witness saw the Defendant in, say, January or February.

If so, this question will be objected to, and the Examiner must proceed to elicit the evidence in another way, for example:—

Q. *Take your mind back to the beginning of this year.*

A. *Yes.*

Q. *Did you see the Defendant then?*

A. *Yes.*

Q. *Can you say which month it was?*

A. *Yes. In January.*

Q. *Do you remember what day of the month it was?*

A. *About the middle of the month.*

Now if the date is *material,* it is obvious that some means must be adopted to bring back to the witness's memory the exact date: that is, if according to his statement he was aware of the date. Those means I will deal with further on, see p. 81 et seq. If the exact date is not material or if the witness never did remember the date, and it cannot be fixed by reference to some other event as indicated on page 81 et seq., the answer must be left for what it is worth. But in no case may the witness be asked: "was it on the 12th of January?" That is obviously a very leading question.

Q. *Did he have an animal in his possession?*

This is an improper question, for of course you are suggesting the answer to the witness.

A. (If question not objected to) *Yes.*

If objected to, then ask: "Did he have anything with him": or "What was he doing at the time," and so on.

Q. *What was the animal?*

A. *An Ox.*

To put the question, "Was it an Ox?" is clearly to put a leading and improper question.

Q. *What was the colour of the Ox?*

This is the proper way to put the question in order to elicit the evidence as to colour. I have heard it put as follows (with variations), in order to "jog" the memory of a dull or forgetful witness: "Was it a white Ox, or black, or what colour?" It may be said that this suggests no answer: but human nature being what it is, it will be noticed in practice that consciously or unconsciously some emphasis is laid on the word "white," and the rest of the question is without emphasis. In this way there is a suggestion made to the witness, and that is not proper.

These questions should, I think, illustrate what is meant by a "Leading Question."

There are some cases where leading questions may be put.

(A)　RULE NOT APPLIED TO FORMAL QUESTIONS.

The rule does not apply to the merely formal parts of the witness's statement. Those are always elicited by means of leading and direct questions: otherwise the case would never be finished. It is when the witness comes to the material points in issue that your opponent will object, with the statement, "Now don't lead him." It is a matter in the discretion of the Judge whether a question is leading or not.

(B)　HOSTILE WITNESS.

If for example your witness appears to be "hostile" to your Client or interested for the other party or unwilling to give evidence, leading questions may be put; in such a case you may even cross-examine him. When a witness may be considered as "hostile" or "adverse" as distinguished from merely "unfavourable," is a question not easy to answer shortly: the *mere fact* that his *answer* is, or even his *answers* are, not in your favour does not necessarily make him *hostile*. But suppose, as happens, that he not only answers unfavourably to you, but of his own accord adds answers, adverse to you, on points on which you have not asked him, and thus shows a deliberate bias and intention of favouring the other party and injuring your Client's case. Such conduct will clearly entitle you to ask that he may be treated as "hostile," and if the Court agrees, then you can cross-examine him. Or suppose he shows an evident reluctance to answer the questions, the answers to which eventually given, after hedging and refusing, are favourable to you; while on the other hand he shows a pronounced alacrity in answering those questions, the answers to which are unfavourable to you, it would be difficult for your opponent to resist the inference that the witness is interested for the other side and unwilling to give evidence for your Client.

DECISION IN ABOVE CASES RESTS WITH THE JUDGE.

In all such cases it must be remembered that the decision whether or not the witness falls under this category rests with the Judge, and not with you.

From this it does not follow that whenever you get merely unfavourable answers it is wise to treat the witness as hostile. It does not do your case any good to have the application refused, with some trenchant comments on its unreasonableness and the perfectly fair way in which the witness is giving his evidence.

(C) INCONSISTENT STATEMENT.

Again, suppose your witness has made at some other time a statement, inconsistent with the evidence which he is giving in the witness-box, and is unfavourable to you.

EXCEPTION TO RULE AGAINST DISCREDITING OWN WITNESS.

It is of course the general rule that you *may not discredit your own witness*, that is, you may not ask questions to show that he is not telling the truth or is not to be believed. What then are you to do in the case put? Ask the Court to hold that the witness is " adverse," i.e., of a hostile mind, and for leave *to contradict him by other evidence* or *to prove that he made such inconsistent statement* at some other time.

How INCONSISTENT STATEMENT MUST BE PUT.

It is in the discretion of the Judge to allow or disallow you to do so: if he allows it, then you can adduce such proof. In the latter case of the inconsistent statement you *must first put the circumstances of the alleged statement sufficient to designate the particular occasion to the witness, and you must ask him whether or not he made such a statement.*

(D)   IDENTIFICATION OF PERSON.

One sometimes hears Counsel say to a witness, where the identification of a person is a material fact, "Look round the Court and say whether you can see the man you are speaking of." But according to the practice in England, which is followed in our Court in matters of evidence, the witness may be told to look at a particular person and say whether he is the man. This certainly *appears* to be a very unfair leading question, because the whole case, civil or criminal, may turn upon the identification of "the man," and naturally when the practitioner on the Witness's side points out a particular person, the suggestion is obvious. But the practice is as I have stated (see Taylor, p. 1178).

(E)   IN CONTRADICTING A WITNESS ON THE OTHER SIDE.

Where a Witness is called to contradict another as to any expression used by the latter (Say X) which he has denied that he has used, then the question may be put directly to the Witness: "Did X say so and so?" But remember that X, when giving evidence, must be asked whether he used the expression. You cannot simply call a witness to depose that X, who has been called for the other party, used such and such expressions without putting them to X.

OTHER EXCEPTIONS TO THE RULE AS TO LEADING QUESTIONS.

Other cases will be found in the books where leading questions have been allowed, but they depend so very much upon the particular circumstances of each case.

(F)   INVOLVED AND COMPLICATED FACTS.

Where the facts are very involved and complicated, more latitude is naturally allowed than where the facts are simple.

(G)   LITTLE CHILDREN.

Leading questions are often allowed to small children, on the ground that the mere placing of them in the witness-box is sufficient to drive every fact out of their heads. On the other hand children are often schooled to tell a tale which naturally requires leading to unfold.

However, the business of the Examiner is to try and get their evidence out of them : it is for the other party to object and for the Court to decide. And the more such evidence can be elicited without objection and overruling the better for your case.

IS AN OBJECTION TO A LEADING QUESTION OF PRACTICAL UTILITY?

It may be said with regard to leading questions that objection raised to them is not of much avail, for the mischief has been done when the suggestive question has been put. That is not correct. Where the action is heard by a Judge or Magistrate of experience, the fact that the answer has been elicited by suggestion will most materially affect the value thereof. It may pass without much comment being made at the time, but the Examiner may rest assured that the evidence has lost the value it would possess if it were stated voluntarily by the witness without any suggestion. Where the action is brought before a Jury, such a breach of the elementary rules of evidence would and should call for sharp admonishment. It may also be pointed out by the Judge to the Jury that the evidence was improperly elicited by means of suggestion, and that its value must be considered in that light. It is a course therefore to be avoided.

REFRESHING THE MEMORY OF A WITNESS.

A Witness has to testify to facts within his own knowledge and recollection, but he is sometimes permitted to refresh his memory by some writing or Memorandum or entry made at the time, or so soon after that the facts were fresh in his memory, by himself or by some person in his presence, *whether such writing is or is not admissible in itself as evidence.* For instance, unstamped receipts are in some cases made inadmissible by Law as evidence: but that does not prevent a witness from looking at his receipt to refresh his memory as to the date, for example. Theoretically the Witness is *not allowed to read out* his notes or the entries, etc. That would be tantamount to producing the notes, etc., as evidence. He has always to give his evidence as being within his own knowledge and recollection. He is therefore supposed to look at his notes, etc., to *refresh* his memory and then give his evidence without looking at them. What witnesses are prone and attempt to do is to read out the notes, etc. The fact that a witness may refresh his memory from writings, which cannot be produced as evidence themselves, shows that this privilege of " refreshing memory " should be strictly confined to his actually refreshing his memory, and should not be extended to his reading out his notes.

In practice it happens that these notes are taken out of his pocket by the Witness as soon as he has been sworn, or they are produced when the necessity arises for the " refreshing of the memory."   As soon as he looks at them, the opposing Counsel will call attention to this, and object.   It then lies upon the practitioner calling him,—if the notes have been made by the witness himself at the time of the occurrence or immediately after, or if made by another person in his presence under such circumstances as to be admissible for the purpose of refreshing the memory (See Taylor)—to prove this.   In the last-mentioned case it is well to prove this by other evidence, if possible before the Witness looks at the notes, etc.

EFFECT OF SUCH NOTES AND REASON FOR CAREFUL EXAMINATION BEFOREHAND.

Now there can be no doubt that the effect upon the mind of an ordinary Juror, of " the man in the street," of producing such notes, though they are theoretically produced merely to refresh the memory, is *practically* the same as if the notes, etc., themselves were allowed to be put in.   And because the Witness may also be " a man in the street," he feels the force of backing up his oral evidence by such notes, entries, etc., and so the entries, etc., often come into existence.

For this reason it is well for you to look carefully into them before they are used to " refresh the memory." (See p. 68).

INSPECTION BY OPPONENT.

For the opposing Counsel is entitled to inspect them, and if he sees anything which will throw doubt upon the truth of the statement that they were made *at the time*, etc., he will make the most of it in Cross-Examination.

He may also cross-examine the Witness respecting such *entries* as have been *previously referred* to in Examination-in-Chief. (See Cross-Examination, p. 106).

If therefore there are any entries in the notes, etc., which you do not desire the Witness to be cross-examined on, that is *as being contained in the notes,* etc., do not let him refresh his memory by looking at those entries.

WHEN NOTES, ETC., CAN BE PUT IN AS EVIDENCE.

Counsel sometimes claim, where the opposing Counsel has cross-examined upon the entries so previously referred to, that the notes, etc., must now be put in on the ground that the opposing party by such examination has made the notes, etc., his own evidence. But that is an untenable claim. Should, however, the opposing Counsel *cross-examine upon any entries to which you have NOT referred in Examination-in-Chief,* i.e., upon which the Witness has merely refreshed his memory by looking at his notes, then the question does arise whether he has not made all the entries as contained in the writing, notes, etc., his evidence, and therefore whether they must not be put in as evidence.

So much then for Leading Questions.

WHERE WITNESS HAS FORGOTTEN A MATERIAL DATE.

And now to revert to the answer given on page 74, where it was *material to fix the exact date* when the Witness saw the White Ox in Defendant's possession, and the Witness stated that he saw the Defendant in the middle of the month. How is he to be got to fix the date without putting leading questions?

REFERENCE TO SOME OTHER FIXED AND ASCERTAINED DATE.

If Counsel has had a conference with Witnesses, he will naturally have elicited from the Witness the why and the wherefore of his being able to fix the particular date in January. As the exact date is of vital importance to the case, it may be assumed that Counsel has used the conference for the purposes for which it is intended. He will also, following the advice given as to noting all amendments, explanations, etc., in his brief in the Witness's statement, have noted the reasons and facts by which the witness identifies the particular date. It is only necessary therefore to direct the attention of the witness to those reasons and facts and his memory will return.

ILLUSTRATION.

To put a case. The day may have been one on which the witness, a farmer, came into the District, Town or Village to attend Nachtmaal, or to consult his Attorney, events which being of peculiar interest to him have become fixed in his memory. Suppose he had come in to attend Nachtmaal, the Examination on page 73 after the answer "in the middle of the month."

Q. *Was Nachtmaal held in the Village of —— in January?*

A. *Yes.*

Q. *Did you attend it?*

A. *Yes.*

Q. *What day of the Month did you go into the Village for that purpose?*

A. *It was on Saturday.*

Q. *Do you remember the date?*

A.   (a) *" Yes, it was the 12th "* or (b) *" it was the second Saturday in the month,"* or (c) *" I don't remember."*

(Either answer will serve the purpose as will appear later.)

Q.   *When was the Nachtmaal Service held?*

A.   *The next Sunday.*

Q.   *Now did you meet the Plaintiff before or after this Nachtmaal Service?*

A.   *It was on the Saturday before: the day I came into the Village to attend the Service.*

Should his answer be in terms of (a), a Calender can be referred to: or, if it be in terms of (b) or (c), *another* witness, who can tell you when the Nachtmaal Service was held, can be asked what the date was. Thus the date of Saturday the 12th can be found as being the day on which the Witness came into the Village and on which he met the Defendant.

Very simple! Yes, if you have taken the preliminary precaution of ascertaining all this beforehand. But how often is this not omitted, and how often does one not find Counsel groping all round for some means of recalling the date to the memory of the Witness.

Chapter XI.

HOW TO EXAMINE YOUR WITNESSES.

———

1. *Let your questions be as short and as simple in language as possible.*

This seems fairly obvious: but there is an exceptional reason in our practice why this rule should be observed.

Additionally so in case of interpretation.

Very much of the examination is done through interpretation. The Interpreter cannot be expected to remember a long and involved question: with the result that something is omitted. Or else the Interpreter interprets at the same time that the question is put: he translates some words spoken by Counsel, then there is a pause: then he translates some more words, and there is another pause: and so on. What the state of mind of the witness is at the end of a long question conveyed in this manner, has often been a matter of speculation and amusement.

In dealing with Country witnesses of little education avoid technical and unnecessary terms, or terms arguing a certain amount of culture, etc. It is interesting to watch some illiterate " By-wooner's" face when Counsel premises, " Now my learned friend asked you if——." A strict Interpreter will say " Mij geleerde vriend ": another will say " Zij geleerde vriend ": and the witness is left speculating whether

Codlin or Short is the "friend": the last thing he dreams of is that opposing Counsel are supposed to be "friends."

AND IN ADDRESSING JURIES IN CRIMINAL CASES.

The habit of using short and simple sentences, especially in cases of interpretation, will be found most useful in addressing the Jury in Criminal defences. You can then feel assured that what you are saying will be conveyed to and understood by them. The latest instance of the result of not observing these apparently obvious but often neglected rules, is the case where a witness was told that he was a "Machiavelli," with a broad "*a*." The interpretation was, "Die Advocaat se jij maak wat jij wil."

2. *Finish the question you are putting* and do not break off half way and put another, which you have forgotten to ask, or which you think should have come before the other. *You* may be able to jump from one incident to another or from one time to another, but the witness must not be expected to. It will only confuse him. But if this is done through *your* fault it seems better to finish one question before putting another—due regard being had to the intelligence of the witness.

3. *Let your witness finish his answer and interrupt him as little as possible.*

Of course, there are occasions when you have to interrupt or stop the witness, especially the garrulous one who will wander off into all kinds of irrelevant matter.

When you have to interrupt him and keep him to the point, do it as gently as you can. Do not be irritable with him: there is sure to be enough of irritation shown by others when the witness plunges into the sea of irrelevancy: but do not let the irritability come from you. This is not as easy as it seems: by no means. When the Bench and your opponents are all displaying obvious and pronounced dissatisfaction with the way your witness is behaving, it is then that you are called upon to exercise your powers of Advocacy, to keep calm and collected, and to *help* the witness as much as possible. The way *not* to do so is to get irritable yourself.

INTERRUPTIONS BY OPPONENT OF HIS WITNESS.

If the practitioner is opposed to the witness who is being examined, he should be on his guard against these interruptions, and carefully watch them. They may be caused by the witness meandering off into hearsay and irrelevant matter: but they may also be caused by the anxiety and fear that he will be saying too much for the side on which he is called.

INTERRUPTIONS BY CROSS-EXAMINER.

Where your witness is being cross-examined, interruptions by the cross-examiner are by no means unusual. It behoves the practitioner on the other side to see to it that answers in his favour are given in full and not stopped in medio.

Then also arises the further danger that you may neglect the next advice, viz., to

4. *Take your time and do not go too fast.*

There *may* be the tendency when the examination is going smoothly to go too fast: but I think there is much more likelihood of doing so when things are *not* going smoothly. Naturally, there is the desire to get rid of the cause of the irritation, and the apparently obvious course is to shorten the examination and get to the central and important point of evidence. But this may not only upset the witness altogether, but may result in the omission of material facts.

By saying "take your time" is not meant that, while avoiding like swift Camilla to skim over the plain, you should like a wounded snake drag the slow length along of the examination.

If the practitioner is clearly of opinion that some evidence is relevant let him bring it out, no matter how unimportant it may seem at the time. It happens more often than seems probable that evidence, apparently of little or no importance at one stage of a case, may later on assume most important dimensions. But then the practitioner must have the ultimate bearing fully before him: otherwise he will obscure his main strong points by a cloud of petty detail.

5. *Where there are well-known matters of discredit to your witness or his character, or there are documents and letters written, or admissions made by your witness and known by your opponent, which cannot be conclusively met,* IT IS BETTER TO DEAL WITH THEM IN THE EXAMINATION in chief than to leave them to be brought out in cross-examination.

The witness may have got into *recent trouble,* a matter known perfectly well to the opposing side; if so, bring it out at the beginning of the examination. Do not adopt the tactics of the proverbial ostrich, and imagine that because you have not faced the fact, your opponents will neglect to bring it into the open. You will find your Client or the witness only too ready to try and hide these facts.

If the trouble is old then say nothing about it, in the hope that your opponent may be foolish enough to do so.

Suppose that the witness has signed some document or letter which ex facie seems against him. In conference (page 49), the witness will have been asked for the explanation. *If the latter is conclusively satisfactory,* then leave it to the opposing side to make what he will of the document, etc. If he omits to give the witness an opportunity of explaining it and contents himself with putting in the document, there is always the opportunity of your doing so in the re-examination: if he does give the witness the opportunity, the conclusive explanation comes with very great force.

If the explanation is not conclusively satisfactory, then get it out in Examination-in-Chief. It is bound to come at some time: and it is better for the witness that it should be elicited in the friendly atmosphere surrounding the practitioner and his witness than in the hostile confusing strain of cross-examination.

CHAPTER XII.

CROSS-EXAMINATION OF WITNESSES.

———

IT MUST be confessed that the cross-examination by the average and inexperienced cross-examiner succeeds in effecting little else than a repetition of what the witness has already said in Examination-in-Chief. And very often with this additional result, that all the strongest points against him have simply been made stronger and more emphatic by the cross-examiner.

The reason for this I believe to be that the latter when he rises to cross-examine *has very little or no idea what course he is going to pursue or what he is going to ask.* That at any rate was my own experience in my early days: and I found it to be the general case with my Juniors also up to my last days at the Bar. Very often it has been put to them: " Now how would you tackle the Plaintiff or Defendant in this case," and the reply has been, " I don't know: I would wait and see what he says." But that is of little avail.

The unfortunate Practitioner beginning his career generally gets up to cross-examine *without any idea of what he should,* or *even of what he is going to ask,* simply because he understands that this is part of his duty. He is expected to do so by his Client and Attorney: and so he does it. If he only had the courage to act in accordance with what he himself often knows only too well, namely, that he may do more harm than good, he would content himself with putting (after having put the necessary questions, see pp. 77, 101) a few harmless questions, and then sitting down. But that would not satisfy his Advisers or his Client. Yet the Client is the very last person who has the least appreciation of the danger of cross-examination—to himself. It is both interesting and amusing to hear some person, who is standing his trial, " Cross-examine " a witness for the Crown. In a very short time he will have removed any doubts as to his guilt which such witness' evidence may have left. If there was a doubt as to the identity of the Criminal with the Accused, he will by his questions show that he was the person: and so on.

But the inexperienced Practitioner may also do almost as much harm to his case. Not only does he make the points against himself stronger and more emphatic by his repetition of the Examination-in-Chief, *but he often lets in evidence* which but for his questions could not be adduced by the other side.

DIFFERENT MODES.

I do not suppose that Cross-examination can be taught; different men have different ways of arriving at the desired end.

THE HECTORING, BULLYING STYLE.

There is the hectoring, bullying mode. This is often effective in what may be called the " Saturday night drunks:" but it will not be of much avail against the educated or commercial witnesses. It is a style which is much encouraged and fostered by the kind of practice the beginner enjoys: namely, pauper divorce suits and defences in petty criminal cases. It is not too much to say that the parties in 90 per cent of the Divorce cases are of the coloured classes, and that in 80 per cent of them the parties are paupers, that is not having £10 in the world. What is an expensive and rare form of litigation among better to do people is quite an everyday indulgence among the lowest coloured classes.

In the petty criminal cases the witnesses are also generally of the lower and humbler classes. With such witnesses the hectoring swaggering form of cross-examination is often effective.

REPEATING THE SAME QUESTION AT DIFFERENT TIMES.

In my early days I thought it a good plan to lead up to and ask the same question in varying forms, several times, and at intervals of time: but it received a somewhat unsympathetic reception, and was crushed by the interjection, " You have already asked that question several times."

PUTTING UNIMPORTANT QUESTIONS AND " SLIPPING IN " AN IMPORTANT ONE.

Then it has been asked: " Do you agree with the advice in the books that the proper way is to ask a number of unimportant questions and then slip in an important one?" Doubtless this may be an excellent way: but it is not easy to see how it is to be done: that is, not as a regular system. If a witness is lying and fencing and can be taken off his guard, the truth may slip out. But as a general rule the average witness does not wilfully make statements devoid of some truth. What usually happens is that the witness through repetition of the story, bias, prejudice and the like, exaggerates and adds a little here and a little there. For a while he will proceed upon the straight and narrow path of the truth as he at least honestly believes it to be: then at some stage instead of continuing this path he will branch off to the right or left, be the deviation much or little.

ALL MODES ARE USEFUL—TACTICS.

Doubtless a master in the art of cross-examination uses all these methods according to circumstances and the personality of the witness: and so he uses the cajoling, laughing, indifferent styles with a humourous facetious witness, especially one who is " playing to the gallery "—it is well to laugh with him, to cajole him, and to put the questions in a tone as if the answer were quite indifferent to you. With another it is excellent policy to hold him up to ridicule.

Will anyone who heard Upington once deal with a Policeman on the " up and down " motion ever forget it? The case was one on Fire Insurance Policies: the defence was Arson and Fraud. A Constable, who had entered the premises (Wine and Brandy stores) before the Fire had got a good hold, described how in a distant corner of the store he saw the flames " rising and falling." Anyone who has noticed the flickering flames arising from spirits with their curious lights and shades will recognise and appreciate the meaning of flames so described. The Constable, after the manner of such witnesses, was rather dramatic in his recital of the " up and down motion." It afforded the opportunity, which was at once seized, of treating the witness by way of ridicule. If the Constable was dramatic, Upington assumed a still more dramatic manner, beginning with great gravity and seriousness, until he had the whole Court, the Bench included, rocking with laughter over " the up and down " motion of the flames.

If as sometimes happens, the witness is somewhat " quicker in the uptake " than the examiner, and instead of being ridiculed rather reverses the position to the palpable enjoyment of the Jury, there seems nothing worse than the assumption of a serious demeanour, rebuking such frivolity. Let the practitioner laugh heartily himself and encourage the witness. The latter becomes so pleased with himself that he becomes silly, and then the Examiner can get a "bit of his own back," or the witness quite forgets that he is on the defensive and lets out much more than he intended. If the practitioner has no sense of humour or of the humorous he had better leave this style of dealing with a witness severely alone.

Every form and style is of use, and it is not possible to say that the beginner must do this or that, and not do something else.

THE STRATEGY.

All the above matters constitute what is conceived to be the "tactics," which necessarily are constantly varying according to the circumstances and characters of the witnesses. Although cross-examination cannot be taught like an exact science, what I do think can be indicated to the reader, is that when he gets up to cross-examine he must have some plan of campaign, *the strategical part: he must or ought to have formed some idea of what he is going to do.* At any rate for what it is worth, that is the method upon which I worked in later years.

THE PLAN MUST BE THOUGHT OUT.

The cross-examination of, at any rate, the principal witness was *not* left to the inspiration of the moment. It was long and carefully thought out, and it was based upon these considerations: "If the witness answers "Yes" to this question, then follow a certain line: if he answers "No" then follow the alaternative line."

What this means it will be attempted to elucidate later on (pp. 117 et seq.).

It enabled the following remark to be made to the witness: "You say so and so: a little while ago you said the contrary: I do not mind which you say, but do make up your mind which it is and stick to it, and let us get on." The effect upon a fencing witness was generally very marked.

THE TACTICS (CONTINUED).

What has been called above the "tactics" of Cross-examination will be dealt with first, not only be it confessed, because it is the easier subject of the two, but because it embraces rules which will prove useful whatever be the strategy employed, and because it may make it easier to understand the strategy.

CHAPTER XIII.

WHAT IS CROSS-EXAMINATION?

———

WHAT IN the first place is cross-examination? I take it that it means, that the witness being called by and being favourable to the opposite side is hostile to your side. Consequently you may contradict and discredit him, you may throw doubt on his veracity, attack his character, show up his motives and interests, and ask him leading questions: all things which you may not do in Examination-in-Chief. He still, however, remains a witness, and his statements constitute evidence. and are therefore subject to the rules of evidence. But the rule that evidence must be confined to the points in issue, and must not include proof of collateral facts from which no reasonable bearing or inference upon the points in issue can be drawn, it not so strictly insisted upon in cross-examination as in Examination-in-Chief.

WHERE WITNESS IS MERELY A FORMAL ONE.

1. This being the basis of cross-examination, it should follow that if a party calls a witness merely to prove some formal fact or documents, which he cannot do without calling the witness, the opposite side should not be allowed to cross-examine him, especially if he be a friendly and favourable witness for the latter.

IN OUR PRACTICE CROSS-EXAMINATION ON *ALL* RELEVANT MATTER IS ALLOWED.

There is no doubt that in our practice a witness may be cross-examined *not only upon the particular points upon which he has given evidence in chief, but upon all or any other points relevant to the case.* But it would manifestly be unfair to allow a witness, who is called only to prove a formal fact which cannot be proved without his evidence, to be treated by the opposite side as a hostile witness when he is nothing of the sort, but quite the contrary: and to elicit his favourable evidence by leading questions.

WHERE A WITNESS IS PARTLY FAVOURABLE AND PARTLY UNFAVOURABLE.

It is of course a difficulty, which has sometimes to be faced in practice, to decide whether or not to call a witness, who is partly favourable and partly unfavourable. But that is quite a different thing from calling a witness to merely prove a formal fact, or to put in some document in his possession. Often, formal facts which should be admitted by the opposite side without the expense and necessity of calling a witness, are refused to be admitted, the idea being to force the witness into the witness-box, and then under the cloak of cross-examination elicit his favourable testimony. But I have known in practice that the Court has refused to allow such a witness to be cross-examined: and in accordance with that practice no cross-examination should be allowed by any Justiciary.

In order to expose such tactics and with an eye to the costs, the opposite side should always be asked in writing to admit such formal fact or document.

WHERE FORMAL WITNESS CALLED ON OPPOSITE SIDE.

It should follow in such a case that if the opposite side subsequently calls that witness as his, he cannot deal with him as on cross-examination. The meaning of this is, that it is said to be in question, *whether the right to cross-examine continues if the cross-examiner recalls the witness as part of his own case.* This very seldom happens. I can only recall one instance, and then the right to Cross-examine was disallowed.

But what does happen sometimes is that after the Plaintiff has proved somewhat formal evidence he closes his case because thereupon the onus is shifted to the Defendant. The latter may be forced to call some witness who, but for the shifting of the onus, would naturally under the circumstances of the case be called for the Plaintiff.

Again, if the above be the true basis of cross-examination, what is the correct position where *a witness called for the opposite side turns out to be hostile to him and he is allowed to treat the witness as hostile.* That means as stated before that the opposite side is then allowed to cross-examine him and attack him and put leading questions to him, etc., as if he were a witness called by his opponent. *But can the Counsel for the party who did not call him also cross-examine and put leading questions to him?* I do not remember that this question has been raised in practice. Where the case is being tried before a Judge it would not make any difference whether such Counsel were or were not allowed to put leading questions: for the answers would have the weight— or the absence thereof—given to them which they deserve. But where the case is being heard before a Jury, it might make a considerable difference.

Even where such a witness has not been actually declared to be and treated as hostile, but shows in cross-examination every eagerness and bias to assist the cross-examiner, is everything favourable to the latter to be allowed to be elicited by leading questions?

These questions are exceptionally important where the case is taken on Appeal. If the evidence taken on the record were in the form of question and answer, the Appeal Court would be in a much better position to judge of the value of the evidence because it would see that it was elicited by a leading question. But in our system of recording evidence by the Stenographers, the questions and answers are not given: indeed, what is often recorded is what in the mind of the Shorthand Writer is the substance and bearing of the question and answer.

So far, however, as the cross-examining practitioner is concerned, it is not his function to decide whether or not such questions may or may not be put. He should put his questions, with due consideration, however, be it noted to the value which he desires to have attached to them. The less the evidence is elicited by the suggestion of leading questions, the more value is likely to be given to the evidence.

2. In cross-examination *leading questions may be put.* But " this does not mean that Counsel can put the very words into the mouth of the witness which he is to echo back again." That is the theoretical limit: in practice it is constantly being exceeded. In fact, in our Courts such an improper practice *has* crept in (following a bad example in re-examination) of putting the words into the mouth of the witness to be assented to or denied by him. The fact that it has no weight whatever with the Court is no reason for the practice, but it affords a good example of what is connoted by the aforesaid limit to putting leading questions. (See Re-examination, page 131.)

BE ON GUARD AGAINST CERTAIN QUESTIONS.

There are two kinds of questions often attempted in Cross-examination which the experienced practitioner immediately stops, but which may not be so obvious to the beginner on the other side. So he is warned to be on his guard.

The one question is, *where some fact which has not been proved is assumed as a fact.*

The other is where it is assumed *that particular answers have been given contrary to the fact.*

They should be objected to at once. The first one is not so easy to detect as the second: naturally. It requires some skill to put it properly. If really analysed it consists of two questions in one: but the first question is stated not as a question but as a fact.

The classical example of the first is the question: "after that did you cease beating your wife," it not having been proved that the witness ever beat his wife. It is often accompanied, when the witness very naturally begins to make an explanation, by the cross-examiner insisting on the witness saying "Answer 'Yes' or 'No'; then you can explain." Of course whether he says "yes" or "no" he admits that he did beat his wife. Again: "What did the Policeman X say to you when you met him?" it not having been proved that the witness did meet the Policeman.

The questions are not always so flagrantly obvious, and therefore the practitioner must be on his guard, and must not allow a question to be put which *assumes* a fact not yet proved.

Suppose the witness has denied in Chief that he met Policeman X and the question is put as above. In this case *a fact is assumed which is contrary to the answers,* and it is assumed that the answer

originally given was that witness did meet the Policeman. This is an example of the second kind of objectionable questions, known colloquially as "catch
questions," and much favoured in certain Lower
Courts.

CONTRADICTION OF A STATEMENT IN CROSS-EXAMINATION.

There is, however, one matter to which attention
should be directed, and that is the cross-examination
of witnesses for the Crown in Criminal cases, who
have made depositions before the Magistrate at the
preparatory Examination. Such witnesses are re-
peatedly asked whether they did not in their depositions make such or such a statement—without anything more: indeed, Counsel often reads the statement from his brief, and leaves it at that. But no
such question can of right be put to such a witness,
nor can he be compelled to answer it, until the deposition has been read by the cross-examiner to the
witness, *and it must be read as part of the evidence
of the cross-examining Practitioner.* The words in
italics constitute the English practice, but it is
seldom insisted on in practice in our Court.

SOME SUGGESTIONS ON THE TACTICS OF CROSS-EXAMINATION.

And now as to some practical suggestions in the
mode of cross-examination.

CHAPTER XIV.

TACTICS.

___

CONTRADICTING OPPONENT'S WITNESS.

If it is intended to contradict a witness called for the opposite party on the evidence which he has given, such witness must be asked questions with regard to the contradictory evidence which will be given. So also if any declarations made by him or acts done by him are to be tendered in evidence to contradict him or impeach his evidence or to show that he is a corrupt witness, the witness *must have his attention drawn to such declarations, and acts, and must be asked whether he made or did them.* In the same way if he is to be contradicted or his evidence impeached by any written document, the latter must first be put to him and *he must be asked whether he wrote or signed it or caused it to be written.*

This emphasizes the necessity of having the brief and the proofs in proper order and sequence so that these points of contradiction, etc., can be readily referred to. And all the more so where the evidence of the witness is to be contradicted on various points by different witnesses who are to be called.

This does not mean that the witness is to be taken over all that he has said in Examination-in-Chief. If he has said that he was *not* present at a certain meeting and evidence is to be tendered that he was, it is not necessary to ask him again if he was present.

But if evidence is to be tendered that, not only was he present at the meeting, but that he spoke and made certain remarks, then he must be asked whether he did not speak and make these particular remarks.

The two guiding rules in the tactics of cross-examination are:

1. DO NOT ASK A DIRECT QUESTION, THE ANSWER TO WHICH MAY BE UNFAVOURABLE TO YOUR CASE.

It is assumed that the practitioner is not going to ask the witness to repeat all that he has said in Chief —for that is not cross-examination—but that he is going to question him on something which will be in conflict therewith, or will modify it, or throw a different light and meaning on it, etc. It must be obvious that to ask such a question *directly* is to court the unfavourable reply. The point must therefore be approached *indirectly*, and the direct question must be avoided. Take a simple illustration. A Plaintiff says that he bought ostriches for farming, and you wish to elicit facts showing that he had no land to graze them on. If you ask him, " had you sufficient land on which to graze them?" he will most probably answer " Yes "—naturally. Instead of doing so you will question him as to the size of his farm, the amount of his arable land, and of grazing land, lucerne land, and so on. Then you elicit how many ostriches he had at the time of the sale. It is assumed that you are instructed how many birds go to a morgen: it was certainly your business to have obtained such instructions before you came into Court. If so, you will be able at once to calculate whether or not there was sufficient grazing for the number of birds alleged to have been bought. If the calculation shows that there was, then you will naturally stop questioning him further on this point: for if you do not stop you will only be strengthening your opponent's case by showing as a fact that Plaintiff could graze the birds.

But if your calculation shows that the land available was not sufficient for grazing the birds alleged to have been bought, then this line of examination can be pursued.

CROSS-EXAMINATION IN FORM OF ASSERTIONS.

And your next question should be in the form of an assertion: viz., " A morgen of grazing or lucerne land will carry X birds?" It should not be, " How many birds can a morgen of grazing or lucerne land carry?" For if it is so put the witness will probably see the drift of the question and go into calculations, with qualifications and modifications. Whereas —it is experience which speaks—if the statement is made as an assertion of a well-known fact, the reply generally is as desired, viz.: in the affirmative.

2. DO NOT CROSS-EXAMINE A WITNESS UPON MATTERS UPON WHICH HE HAS NOT SAID ANYTHING IN EXAMINATION-IN-CHIEF, UNLESS YOU ARE VERY SURE, INDEED, OF YOUR GROUND.

The only reason for cross-examining in this case is in order to elicit evidence favourable to your own side. Of course, if your instructions are clear and definite that he will give favourable replies, the opportunity should not be missed. But can you rely on this being the case: if you cannot, it is far better to leave the witness alone.

Sometimes it is thought that the witness must be favourable to the Cross-examiner or otherwise the evidence omitted would have been given in Examination-in-Chief. But that does not necessarily follow. His evidence on the points on which he was silent may in fact have been *partly favourable* and *partly unfavourable* for the party calling him, and the latter has wisely asked him no question on these points, preferring to prove them by some witness who is wholly favourable.

And here let it be noted *that questions in the form of assertions of fact are sometimes the very best means of eliciting the real facts from a witness.* Instead of saying to a witness, " Did you then do so and so?" the cross-examiner says, " And then you did so and so?" putting himself mentally in the position of an eye-witness. If with any such question he strikes a fact, it is extraordinary how often he can lead the witness along the line which that fact points to.

WHEN WITNESS BECOMES RELUCTANT.

As the latter gets nearer and nearer to some fact which will materially conflict with his evidence-in-Chief, he may, seeing where he is being led to, begin to be reluctant. Then comes the difficulty to the cross-examiner: *how far shall he press the witness!* If he is pressed too far he will answer in the negative, just where it would have been better for the cross-examiner *not* to have had such answer. On the other hand he might with further pressure have given an affirmative answer. It is wiser when the witness begins to " jib "—to put it colloquially—*not* to press him further. In other words, " Leave well alone," perhaps the most difficult advice of any to follow.

On the other hand if you have led him on so far that it is immaterial whether he answers in the affirmative or negative: that is, if his answer in the negative would be contradictory of or inconsistent with something which he has already said, then there is not only no danger in pressing him, but it is a wise thing to do so. Because the result, if he gives such a negative answer, is that he is shown to be untruthful or forgetful, etc.

The next guiding rule is,

3. BE CAREFUL NOT TO ASK QUESTIONS WHICH WILL ALLOW THE OPPOSITE SIDE TO PUT IN MATERIAL EVIDENCE WHICH HE COULD NOT PUT IN IN CHIEF.

Take an illustration. Suppose the witness called for the Plaintiff has had a material conversation with the Plaintiff when your Client, the Defendant, was not present. That conversation cannot as a rule—because there may be exceptions, e.g., if the witness was a general agent, etc.,—be elicited in Chief. Now under ordinary circumstances not even a beginner would be so unwise as to ask questions as to what was said at this conversation. But it sometimes happens that there are letters or documents written by the witness, which to the mind of the cross-examiner contain some statements which appear inconsistent with such conversation being in favour of the Plaintiff's case. The Cross-examiner concludes that if such conversation were elicited it would be in his favour. So he puts questions about what was said, believing that if the answers are unfavourable he will be able to show up the witness by confronting him with the letter or document. Now this may sometimes be the case: but by asking questions about the conversation, the whole of it is let in : i.e., the opposite side can now put in the whole conversation.

But this is always a dangerous step, and one to be avoided, to let in evidence—you cannot tell how very unfavourable it may be—in the *hope* or *expectation* of eliciting something which is favourable.

How much better and safer it is, in the case put, to wait until the address takes place, and then to point to these letters or documents as containing expressions favourable to one's Client.

When may a document put in Cross-examination be seen.

The question when the practitioner is entitled to see a document put into the hands or produced by a witness when examined in Chief is dealt with on p. 80-1.

It may be well to deal with the point: when is the practitioner entitled to see a document shown to one of his witnesses by the Cross-examiner. It is thus stated by Taylor (Section 1452): the cases are somewhat conflicting, but the practice seems to be as follows: if the cross-examiner after putting a paper into the hands of a witness merely asks him some question as to its general nature or identity, or respecting the character of the hand-writing, his adversary will have no right to see the document: but if the paper be used for the purpose of refreshing the memory of the witness, or if any questions be put respecting its contents, a sight of the paper may be demanded.

Where the witness has relied on some writing or document alleged to have been made at the time.

Assuming that the writing or document is not in itself admissible as evidence, for example, if it be a diary kept by the witness, the latter can refresh his memory by looking at the writing. Suppose it is a date of some event like a wedding which is of importance in establishing an alibi, it is somewhat absurd to imagine that the witness who is called in order to establish the alibi requires to look at the diary to refresh his memory. The real reason is to convey the impression that as the *note was made at the time* it is likely to be correct, especially if at *that time* there was no idea of the necessity of establishing an alibi: and such is undoubtedly the impression which *is* conveyed let the technical and theoretical rule be what it may. If therefore the value of the entry can be weakened, it certainly should be. If it be a genuine entry there is no more to be said: but suppose it is not: what are the particular points to be looked for in order to cross-examine with a view to breaking down the value of such entry?

The object, of course, is to show that the entry was made *at a time later* than that on which it purports to be or is alleged to have been made: if that can be done, the question at once suggests itself, why should the witness have as an afterthought made the entry and ante-dated it if his story was an honest and truthful one—and so does the answer!

The writer of the diary will naturally have attempted to insert the entry under the proper date, and will, if necessary and possible, have erased some other writing to find room for the entry, but what often happens is that the entry has to be *cramped* somewhat to make it fit in. Sometimes the entry does not follow in chronological sequence. On other occasions a different ink has been used. It has happened also that the paper on which the writing has been written is such that it *could not have been available at the time* and place when the writing is alleged to have taken place.

Such are some of the most usual means by which the Cross-examiner can break down the evidence of entries, etc., not made at the time alleged.

There is a popular idea that typewritten documents are all of a sameness, and that, for example, forgeries by means of type-writing are not discoverable like forgeries in hand-writing. There is no greater delusion. Type-writers have their own individualities, peculiarities, and idiosyncrasies just as hand-writing has: and it will be found difficult to get two typewriters of the same make which type *alike*. Further,

Typists show their individuality in typing as Pianists do on a Piano.

The investigation into typing and typewriters has been carried to great lengths in America, where very complete and thorough Treatises have been written on these subjects.

As to Accepting Suggestions during Cross-Examination.

The cross-examining Practitioner should be very careful as to accepting suggestions on these or any other points from his client. It is astonishing how often one hears from the Client "Vra ver hem...... hij kannie ontken nie." "Ask him so and so......... he can't deny it." And this is even confidently said upon points, which, if they were not denied, would leave the side calling the witness with no case at all, or would argue a high degree of mental aberration in calling the witness. These risks and dangers do not exist to anything like the same degree in Criminal trials as in Civil suits. For in the former the cross-examiner has the deposition before him made at the Preparatory Examination, and he can therefore ascertain whether the witness has given evidence on any of the points on which he has not been asked at the trial. If he has, then elicit them. But if he has not, then leave them alone, unless, e.g., you have a signed statement of fact to the contrary.

These considerations give rise in natural sequence to the following:

4. Be very careful indeed how you accept any suggestion of putting a question from anyone in the course of or at the end of your cross-examination.

Practitioners sometimes do as much harm to their cases by not observing this rule as in any other way. The reason is very obvious—if one has had the sad experience. The whole of your mind and attention are being given to pursuing a certain train of thought. Suddenly, either in the course of such train or when you have followed it to the end so far as your mind goes, a suggestion is made to you. There is no time to think over it before putting the question: indeed, your mind is not in a proper condition to weigh it. As well as you can you do weigh it: it seems a proper question and quite innocent and without risk, so the question is put—and often fatally put. A few minutes later when you are in a proper condition you look at the question properly, and you would give the world to recall it.

It should be apparent that the putting of questions in this way must be attended with great risk. If the question is of any importance, it is not probable that you would have overlooked it. I can remember occasions when such a suggestion was made, and the following was the train of thought: " It is not strange or unfamiliar to me—if it were I should take no notice of it—it must therefore have been present to my mind at some time, and I must have overlooked asking it." The question was put: only to realize a moment thereafter that the question *had* been considered and weighed, and that I had determined *not* to ask it because it was too dangerous. And the very thing I had resolved *not* to do I had in the stress and strain of cross-examination *done*, and the danger I had anticipated was actually there. No: dangerous as it is to accept suggestions without the most careful consideration *before* the trial, I would advise the inexperienced Practitioner not to accept any during his cross-examination. They may be very good: if so, they would probably have been made before the trial: if they have only been born during the course of his cross-examination in the mind of the suggestor, they cannot have been properly weighed. When the cross-examiner is old, experienced, and cool, this is another matter, but it always, in my opinion, remains a very risky one.

5. BE CAREFUL TO GET AN ANSWER TO YOUR QUESTION AND DO NOT LET THE WITNESS DRAW YOU OFF INTO A SIDE OR MINOR ISSUE.

Always keep your objective in view when you have asked a question, so that you get an answer to *it*. It is presumed that you have an objective in view, and are not merely groping round in the hope of finding something, in which case you will very probably be led astray.

It is very interesting to watch and notice how a clever witness will lead the cross-examiner into some side or minor issues. He may do this either to get him away from the point altogether, or to gain time so that he may consider how to answer the question. The method generally adopted is to give a sort of half answer with a reference to some other or less important fact or issue: or he will retort by asking a question which again refers to some other issue. What then sometimes happens is, that the cross-examiner follows up this *other* issue, and in doing so *omits* or *forgets* to pursue his *original* objective.

When a witness is found doing this, often accompanied with a show of indignation or an apparent burst of candour, it may be assumed that the question is an awkward one for the witness, and therefore there is all the more reason why the examiner should not be drawn away from it to some other issue.

There is, however, quite a well-known and common type of witness whose method of answering most questions, especially awkward ones, is to break out into a stream of volubility. It is what is vulgarly described as " Talking you blind," and is one not uncommon on the Country side in commercial transac-

tions with the farming community. All the talking
is done by the one party, with such volubility that the
other man does not know if he is on his head or on
his feet, and his mind is in a hopeless confusion as
to the terms of the contract which he enters into.

Some Practitioners interrupt such a witness and
keep on trying to bring him back to the point; but it
is no easy matter to stop this stream of utterances,
and in the midst of this altercation with the witness
it is quite as likely that the Examiner will be diverted
into some side issue as that the witness is brought to
the point. And that certainly is the object of the
witness in most cases, if he is not merely playing for
time. But I would advise the Examiner not to interrupt him: let him give free vent to his volubility.
And for this reason. He cannot always consider and
weigh what he is saying, and it sometimes happens
that in this volubility he says more than he intended.
Listen carefully, therefore, to what he is saying, and
when you hear something of importance to the case,
which has " slipped " out, though it may not bear on
the *question you have put,* make a careful mental
note of it, or write it on your brief, or get your Junior
to do so if you have one. *But do not be diverted into
dealing with those points then.* When the witness
has ceased his flood of talk, repeat your original
question, and make it clear to him that you mean to
have an answer to that question, no matter how he
may fence with it. You will deal with the note,
mental or written, of the evidence which has
" slipped " from him at the proper time: and as he
may not be fully aware of what has slipped from him
in his volubility, you will be able to surprise him
somewhat when you confront him afterwards with
these " slips."

6. WHEN YOU HAVE GOT AN ANSWER FAVOURABLE TO
YOUR SIDE FROM A WITNESS, REST CONTENT AND LEAVE
WELL ALONE, AND DO NOT REPEAT THE QUESTION TO
OTHER WITNESSES.

This may be best illustrated by an actual experience. The lower proprietors on a river enjoyed the
right to take out a dam and servitude furrow on an
upper proprietor's farm. A flood washed away the
dam in the river, which served to divert the water
into the furrow. The lower proprietors maintained
that it was impossible to repair such dam and entrance, and claimed another place somewhat higher
up. The upper proprietor was insolvent, and his
trustee maintained that that former entrance could
be repaired, and that it was the most convenient spot
for the dam on the upper farm, which had been mortgaged to a Creditor, a bank. The lower proprietors
brought an action against the trustee. After the leading lower proprietor had given evidence, describing
the insuperable difficulties of repairing or using the
former dam and entrance of the furrow, and the absence of any inconvenience to the upper farm in shifting such dam and entrance higher up, the late Chief
Justice said in effect to him: " But, Mr. Olivier, if
that is so, can you suggest why the trustee should
oppose and contest this action which will evidently
be a costly one." The witness could suggest no
reason.

Another witness was then called, and after his Examination-in-Chief to the same effect, the late James
Leonard, who had then not had much experience in
the practical part of the profession, rose to cross-
examine, and at once repeated the same question to
the witness: " Now can you, Mr. ——, suggest," etc.
The witness could suggest no reason. The Court then
adjourned for lunch. In the interval the Junior for

the Plaintiffs said to the witness who was to be called next, and who was about the most influential and the shrewdest man in the District, and not a Plaintiff: "Mr. G., what will be the result if the Plaintiffs cannot take out their furrow higher up?" and he replied, "I can see no other help for it, but they will have to buy the upper farm." Said the Junior: "It is fully mortgaged to the Bank, is it not?" to which G. replied, "Fully mortgaged! I should think so: it is mortgaged for a great deal more than it would fetch in the market." To this the Junior said: "Then the Plaintiffs will have to buy at the Bank's own price?" "Quite so," was the answer.

After lunch, G. was called as a witness, and when his Examination-in-Chief was finished, Leonard rose, apparently thinking that he had got hold of a most excellent point—which it was, if well had been left alone—repeated the question to G.; "Now, Mr. G., can *you* suggest," etc. "Yes," said G., "I think I can;" and he proceeded to point out that the Plaintiffs would have to buy the upper farm at the Bank's, the Creditor's, own price.

The possible motive was made apparent. But if the Cross-examiner had been content to "leave well alone" after the question had been put by the Bench, there is no knowing what the effect might not have been.

All this may seem very simple; but it is only too well-established a fact that when the inexperienced Practitioner has got hold of a good point, he becomes so fascinated by it, that he finds it almost impossible to leave it alone, and he worries at it, until what with an explanation here and a suggestion there, all the "point" is rubbed off.

7.   AVOID AS MUCH AS POSSIBLE THE QUESTION, "THEN HOW DO YOU EXPLAIN.....?"

Presumably when this question is asked, the cross-examiner has put the witness in the position of having made statements either contradictory to or irreconcilable with some other statement made by him or by some other witness: otherwise it is difficult to see the object of the question. But if that is so, why should the Cross-Examiner even give the witness the opportunity to explain. That is no part of his case. His business is to elicit answers on questions of fact from the witness and to comment on them when addressing the Bench or Jury. By asking for an explanation the Practitioner, of course, thinks that the witness cannot give one, and the question is generally put in a tone of voice which means "You can't explain." But unfortunately for him the witness does sometimes explain when the contradiction is put before him in this clear way: and explains it too in a manner which demolishes the whole of the cross-examination. The temptation is hard to resist: you think you have the witness in a tight place, it may be by answers given at some intervals of time: instead of keeping the idea to yourself, out it must come, and triumphantly you cry: "You said so and so: but you also said so and so: now how do you explain it?"....... and the witness *does!*

No: do not give him the opportunity to explain: Comment on the inconsistency or contradiction in your address. "Oh," it is objected, "but the witness's counsel may get him to explain." Very well: what of it? If the explanation is so simple then it will be given when you *invite* the witness to explain: if the witness *cannot* give an intelligent explanation, then you can realize the scene when *his* Counsel is trying to get him to give one!

Equally dangerous and unnecessary is the question heard so often from beginners:

"CAN YOU SUGGEST WHY THE PLAINTIFF AND HIS WITNESSES SHOULD COME HERE AND COMMIT PERJURY?"

The danger is illustrated in Rule 7, viz., that the witness *may be able* to do so. But I would bring home to the practitioner the futility of it. Why should you give the witness the opportunity of saying in cross-examination what he has not said, and may not be entitled to say, in Examination-in-Chief. If he were to make some very damaging statements against your Client or his witnesses, which might be quite untrue, you may not have the opportunity to contradict him, e.g., if you are for the Plaintiff and are cross-examining the Defendant's witnesses. One knows that the Cross-examiner thinks that by this form of question he is making and emphasizing a good point—if it comes off. But it may not come off: and it is bad advocacy to run these unnecessary risks. Unnecessary because the same point can be made and brought out fully in the address to the Jury. And hence the main and governing rule in Cross-examination:

DO NOT PUT DIRECT QUESTIONS, THE ANSWERS TO WHICH MAY BE UNFAVOURABLE TO YOU.

To which may be added further:

DO NOT ASK QUESTIONS, THE ANSWERS TO WHICH CANNOT BE CONTRADICTED.

In cross-examining as to the character of a witness,

8. BE CAREFUL THAT HIS CRIMINAL OR DISHONEST ACT BE OF RECENT DATE.

In my salad days I asked a witness, a broker, without having previously ascertained all the facts, whether he had not been convicted of fraud.   The witness (now long dead) admitted it, but said " it took place ten years ago," and he made a feeling appeal to the Court as to the cruelty of the question, pointing out how since then he had worked hard and honestly, and had built up a considerable business which entailed the confidence and trust of those who employed him.   This roused all the indignation and sympathy of the Bench, and it seemed to me that this single question had more to do with my Client losing the case than anything else.   Of course, if the witness has been guilty of a *repetition* of dishonesty, that is quite a different matter.

CHAPTER XV.

THE STRATEGY OF CROSS-EXAMINATION.

THE STRATEGY of cross-examination, as I conceive it, is that the Cross-examiner, when he rises, *has some clear conception in his mind as to the course which he intends to pursue, and the objective which he is going to aim at.* It will be attempted to illustrate the method in which such a course was mapped out and the objectives determined. The case taken will be that put on page 36 et seq., viz.: that your Client, the Plaintiff, sues for the purchase price of certain Ostriches alleged to have been sold to the Defendant, delivery to be made in a month's time, and that the plea is a denial that any sale was concluded. It is chosen because ex facie it will not appear to the young Practitioner as one which admits of much planning, especially as it is assumed that there were no instructions, or practically none, briefed which supply any material for cross-examination.

The first point to be noticed from the pleading is that the *Defendant was ready and willing to negotiate for the sale.*

Even if the pleadings merely denied the sale, this inference may be drawn. Of course, if the whole story told by the Plaintiff is a fabrication, and there is no foundation of truth in his statement or justification for his action, then there is an end to the whole matter. The practitioner cannot be expected to win the case with no cards in his hand, and no brilliancy of play any more than the greatest brilliancy in cross-examination is going to make one win the tricks or the Law suit. So one must start with the assumption that there is some foundation for the Plaintiff's case, and that being so, the deduction follows that the Defendant did enter into some negotiations in regard to the sale.

It is assumed, in order not to complicate matters too much, that the price was the ruling market price.

It is clear that in this case, what has to be sought for are the *motives* which make the Defendant repudiate the contract.

Now the Defendant, having been willing to buy and ex hypothesi *would* have bought because he was willing to negotiate, must have been in a position, or able to place himself in a position, to use land for the purpose of grazing the birds—unless he was a mere speculator and not an Ostrich Farmer: and he must in the same way have been in a position, or able to put himself in a position, to pay the price.

The first alternatives are therefore that he was either a Speculator or an Ostrich Farmer. Let each alternative be taken.

If he was a mere speculator, without land of his own, then he must have contemplated selling the birds and as speedily as possible. For it would soon prove a profitless speculation if grazing had to be sought and paid for. Moreover, he had only a month before payment became due, and he would naturally endeavour to sell the birds before the expiration of the month.

Now if the Practitioner has done anything at all in getting up the case, he will at least have ascertained whether the market has gone down within that month and was lower at the date of delivery than at the time of the sale: if it was, then there is an obvious and substantial reason for the repudiation of the sale by the purchaser, a speculator—and one objective is attained.

If the market remained the same, then the only reasonable alternative is that the Defendant tried to resell the birds and could not succeed: thus that becomes the objective to be aimed at.

But if the Defendant was not a Speculator but a Farmer of Ostriches, then there is the other alternative to be followed up, viz.: he must have had land for grazing, or if he had none then he must have had some idea that he would be able to secure sufficient for grazing.

If on questioning him, not, of course, directly, but indirectly, as pointed out in "Tactics" (p. 102), it appears that *he had sufficient land,* then it is clear that this line must be abandoned, and the Cross-examiner must fall back on the line of the Defendant's financial position.

If it appears that *he had not sufficient land* then a substantial motive for repudiation is obtained, unless he *tries to make out the case that he could have obtained such land.*

In which event he must be made to give the names and farms, etc., of the persons from whom he says that he could obtain such grazing, and the reasons why he states that he could obtain it from such persons. If a wire be immediately sent to make enquiry from the persons whose names are given, and the reply shows that the statements are without foundation, the witness may be asked to be recalled. But it will often be found that if the witness be asked fully for such names, etc., and they are deliberately written down, one by one, as he stands in the witness-box, he will see where he is drifting to, and if his statements are baseless, he *will begin to hedge.* He can then be driven on to the horns of a dilemma: *either he had some idea when he negotiated where he could get land or he had none.* If he had, then he must have failed to get the land: if he had none, then his story comes to this; that though willing to negotiate and to buy, and but for some want of agreement as to price or the like he *would* have bought, yet he had made no preparation, or conceived no idea where to graze them. q.e.a.

To revert to the position which unfolds itself, if the Defendant had sufficient grazing. It is clear, as stated before, that this line must be abandoned, and the Cross-examiner now takes up the alternative which arises upon the question of his financial position.

As he negotiated for the sale, and but for some want of agreement upon price or conditions or the like, *would* have bought the birds, he *must have been in a position to pay for them or conceived that he could have made some financial agreement to pay for them*: and the Cross-examiner proceeds to deal with these points.

In actual practice it will not be necessary to pursue all these alternatives, especially if the Practitioner has given heed to the suggestions to be found on pages 36 et seq. He will have acquired some knowledge of the actual state of affairs: thus he will know whether the Defendant is a mere Speculator or a Farmer of Ostriches, and therefore he will discard at once certain of the alternatives indicated above. But they are all set out so as to illustrate what the Practitioner should map out for himself, so that he has before him the particular objective which he is aiming at when he puts a question, and does not ask questions without clearly realizing the why and wherefore of his cross-examination.

This is an illustration of the method employed where the Practitioner appears for the Plaintiff. The same principles apply when he cross-examines on behalf of the Defendant. But the working out is simpler: because the plaintiff's case is that a sale did take place, for he is actually suing to have it carried out, and therefore *the motives actuating him are still existing*. If they were no longer in existence, he would not be desirous of forcing the alleged sale, and obtaining a Judgment for damages as well.

The Practitioner will proceed to analyse the alternatives in the same way.

The Plaintiff is either a Speculator or a Farmer of Ostriches. If he is the former, it is naturally his business to try and sell the birds as soon as possible. Now starting with the same hypothesis that there were negotiations for the sale which were *not* concluded, what are the possible motives which actuate the Plaintiff in maintaining that the unconcluded sale was really concluded.

It is apparent that in a case such as this, it is the *motives* that must be sought for: therein differing from a case such as injury sustained through negligent driving where that which has to be sought for are the *reasons* for the exaggerations of the witness such as bad light, a position from which the witness could not properly see what had happened, etc.

The first alternative naturally is that the market has gone down, for then there is an obvious and substantial reason for the action.

If the market has remained the same, there may be fewer buyers and greater difficulty in selling: or the Plaintiff may have tried after the negotiations were broken off, to sell to others: and so on in the same way.

If the Practitioner has followed the suggestions advising enquiries into all these matters when advising on evidence and has made due and proper use of the conference with witnesses, he will, of course, have information on some of the alternatives which will render their being examined upon wholly un-necessary. But for the residue, he will at any rate when he gets up to cross-examine *know what he is going to aim at and what he is going to try to elicit.* His cross-examination will be greatly shortened, it will be definite, and not a mere rambling repetition of the Examination-in-Chief.

This method of working out the strategy—viz., if he answers " Yes," then what line must be taken, and if he says " No," then what is the alternative, was adapted to the ever varying forms of action. Take the case of a collision, of an accident, of any case founded on negligence. There are in all such cases certain crucial landmarks, e.g., the light, the position of the witness, his greater or less facility for obser-vation, speed, etc., etc. In all these questions, the weight of the evidence naturally depends on what the witness answers, and the problem before the Cross-examiner is to determine what objective he shall make for if the witness answers one way or the other.

Take the question of speed in a collision: the Plain-tiff will be fairly sure to make that of the Defendant excessive: the Defendant will naturally reduce it. If the former is to be cross-examined, the problem is what questions are to be asked in order to reduce the speed, which is the objective to be aimed at. This must be thought out. Distances are measured, time is taken into account, and the actions of the parties during the alleged time that passed are considered. If the speed is stated to be so and so, then could the actions be performed in the time: and so on. And some very hard thinking is sometimes required to determine what line to adopt should the answer be in a certain form. But without it, it is difficult to conceive how the Cross-examiner can possibly decide what his aim and object in putting his questions are to be, or how he is to attain his objective.

It will be found of the greatest use in cross-examination if the Practitioner has prepared the material in the way suggested in advising on evidence, and in his conferences with his witnesses. It is not enough to make his own case clear: he must try and anticipate his opponent's case: by which I do not mean that the plaintiff, e.g., must call evidence in anticipation of the defendant's case—but to anticipate it so that enquiries can be made and evidence and material collected to meet it, and for the purposes of cross-examination: and never more so than when his own case seems to be so clear that *the opponent appears to* have no case at all.

Perhaps I may be allowed at the risk of a charge of egotism to refer to an incident in Cross-examination which may illustrate some of the suggestions which I have ventured to give on Cross-examination. I have forgotten the incident, though not the case itself, but it is referred to in the Law Journal—so I accept it as accurate.

The Plaintiffs were suing for several thousands of pounds as damages for breach of contract in not making delivery of stock. The action had reference to some of the " loot " Cattle taken in the Matabele War, most of which ultimately died through Rhinderpest. A large number of these " loot " cattle had been sold to the Imperial Cold Storage Company by the Chartered Company, but not delivered. The Court found eventually that the Defendant Company had committed a breach of their contract, (of which speaking from memory there was not much doubt) in not delivering the cattle. They had mostly, if not all, died of Rhinderpest, so that delivery was not possible, and the main question apart from the breach, was that of damages.

The Secretary for the Plaintiffs gave considerable evidence on the contract, correspondence, etc. He

was a shrewd and able business man. On rising to
cross-examine I said to him in effect, "It seems to
me you were very lucky in not getting delivery of
the cattle," to which he replied, "Yes, we were
rather." *Upon that I sat down.* The reader will appreciate that this was a big and important Law suit
between two rich and powerful institutions, and that
a good many thousands were at stake. The witness
was, as I have said, a shrewd and capable business
man, well able to hold his own against most Counsel
I have ever heard deal with witnesses. His evidence
had been material and full. I have no doubt that
my Clients expected a long and searching cross-examination: and there is little doubt, if any, in my mind,
that had I been a beginner (it is very improbable that
I would have led in that case: but leaders do fall ill
sometimes), all the above factors would have exerted
sufficient pressure to have induced such cross-examination.

The suggestions made and advice given as to Cross-
examination may be applied to this case so far as applicable. It may be assumed that the alternative
line had been thought out in case the witness had
answered in the negative. By the answer, which contained the admission that so far from having sustained damage from the breach they had been saved
loss thereby, the objective aimed at by the question
was attained: viz.: the minimising of the damage.
For if delivery had been made the Plaintiffs would
have had to pay for the stock, and would then almost
certainly have lost them through the Rhinderpest:
hence their luck in not getting delivery.

Looking at the examination quite dispassionately
—for as I have said I do not remember this incident,
though I do remember the case and the Secretary—I
think it will be found that it follows the advice, etc.,
I have ventured to suggest. Often so easy to give and

so hard to follow oneself. It is at any rate a good
example of the application, in the presence of great
temptation and pressure to do otherwise, of the best
of all advice, viz.: of " Leaving well alone," and of

CHAPTER XVI.

CRIMINAL DEFENCES.

———

IN DEALING with a civil suit before a Judge or Magistrate, it will not avail the practitioner much to elicit and labour a number of small inconsistencies. But it is a different matter where a person is being tried on a criminal charge. There the accused is entitled to the benefit of the doubt, and everything which goes to throw doubt on a witness' testimony may be legitimately brought out and strongly commented upon. Having the depositions before him, the practitioner can call attention to all discrepancies between the evidence of the witness as given before the Magistrate and at the trial, and to all the omissions or additions in such evidence. Indeed, in most cases that fall to the young practitioner that is about all that he can do.

There is one consideration to which his advocacy might be directed, which seems to me has not sufficient attention paid to it. It is the way in which testimony which is not quite certain upon some particular point (or points: but this is rare) before the Magistrate has become more definite at the trial. The witness during the interval will have discussed the details of the crime with the other witnesses, although they will always deny having done so. It always seems such a futile question for the defending practitioner to ask a witness whether he has talked to the other witnesses about the incidents of the alleged crime. Of course, he denies it. Why not take it for granted. Jurors are not fools: and you have only to put it to them how the neighbours must of necessity have been gossiping about what to them is a *cause celebre*, and comparing notes, and disputing about the accuracy of their different versions and convincing each other of discrepancies; they will see that this must naturally be so. The canvas being thus prepared, you should then deal with some evidence in the deposition and at the trial, to illustrate what has actually taken place. You should therefore be on the watch for any such "stiffening" of the evidence. It must always be borne in mind that the depositions cannot convey the hesitation or doubt expressed in the manner of the witness. It is therefore necessary to read between the lines, and still better to visualize the attitude and manner from the language of the deposition. The latter for example reads: "Yes, I think he had on a blue suit." In itself nothing much. But visualize if you can what the attitude may have been; for it may contain a world of meaning. The "Yes" may have been long-drawn out as if said during much thinking. The "I" might also have been drawn out as if the witness was not sure of his answer: and there may have been emphasis laid on the word "think:" the whole expressing the real doubt which did exist in the witness' mind. Now suppose that at the trial the witness has answered without hesitation, "He had on a blue suit." Contrast such a statement with what has been suggested above, and it should become apparent what a sound foundation for creating a doubt as to the witness' evidence has been established. Yet over and over again the Defending practitioner has done no more than draw attention to the fact that in the deposition the witness said "I think," at the trial he was positive.

In the latter case the effect glides off, there is so much for the Juror to take in—but in the former case you may have the satisfaction of seeing a Juror's face light up and his head give a nod or two as if he were saying: "Yes, by Jove, that is so." So pay some attention to any signs in the evidence of this stiffening.

Children are the most difficult to deal with. I could never see the use of asking a child, "Did your mother tell you to come and say so and so?" If the story is a "got-up" one, you may be quite sure that the one thing that the mother has done is to warn the child that if she is asked if her mother told her to say so and so, she must answer "No;" and she answers "No," and you create the impression that the child is telling the truth and the whole truth. Is it not much better to appeal to the common sense of the Jury that the child must of necessity have heard her mother talk of the incidents, etc.?

The only way that suggested itself to me in practice in dealing with a child, is to begin with some questions which have no direct bearing on the main incidents, and try to be as gentle and "parental" as you can. Whatever you do, do not bully or frighten her: she may be the most consummate little liar, but she is a child, and the sympathy is all with her. Question her upon anything which has only an indirect bearing, which leaves her "guessing," and which it is improbable would have been thought of by the mother: that is, if the story has been made up, and polished and polished till all its different parts fit like a mosaic—in the centre. The borders of the pattern will not have been thought of—but it is just such borders which may throw the whole pattern into disharmony.

The Country practitioner is often faced with the problem in defences of accused persons, whether to disclose his defence or not, and whether to cross-

examine freely or not, and if not, then to what extent.
I will give the reasons that actuated me in practice
so that the practitioner may judge for himself and
follow them or not as he thinks fit.

DISCLOSING FULL DEFENCE.

Unless the object of the defence is to induce the
Magistrate to discharge the accused after the preliminary, *or* to turn the case into a summary one, *or*
to induce the Attorney-General not to prosecute, I
cannot see any advantage whatever in disclosing the
full defence, which includes the calling of the witnesses for the accused, save the small one of pointing
out to the Jury that your witnesses have told the
same tale at the trial as they did at the Preliminary
and that the defence is not an after thought—that is,
if and when your witnesses *have told the same tale*.
For they, of course, are also liable to cross-examination and to be confronted with their depositions before the Magistrate, and may therefore also " commit " inconsistencies and contradictions. They may
be less liable to do so, because *they* will no doubt
have had copies of their depositions supplied to them
—(although it must not be supposed that witnesses
for the prosecution have not their memories somewhat refreshed) : still, they may be broken down or
shaken just as witnesses are in civil cases.

This little advantage, pointed out, by no means
compensates for the disadvantage of having your witnesses confronted with the depositions : so that except
in the cases mentioned above, viz., of obtaining a discharge, etc., there is no good to be got by disclosing
the defence. The moment you have done so, the police
will seek—and quite justifiably—for evidence to
break down the defence.

Now it does not often happen that an accused is
discharged by the Magistrate, at any rate not in
serious cases : though doubtless it is more often the

case that the Attorney-General declines to prosecute.
Whether this is likely or not in any particular case,
it is impossible to suggest unless all the facts were
before one. But as a general rule and in the majority
of cases it is wiser not to depend on either a discharge
or a nolle prosequi, and therefore it is better *not* to
disclose the defence at the Preliminary. So far as
Counsel is concerned he will not even have the satisfaction of receiving the gratuitous advertisement
"that Mr. Attorney X has been informed by the Attorney-General that he declines to prosecute in the
case of R. vs. Klaas Geswint charged with cellar
breaking and theft": though should the Attorney-
General decide to prosecute even when the defence
has been disclosed, and the client is found guilty,
Counsel may have the melancholy satisfaction—which
will most certainly not be advertised—of knowing
that the case was lost through the mistake of disclosing the defence at the Preliminary Examination.

CROSS-EXAMINATION AT THE PREPARATORY.

Having decided not to disclose the defence, the
question arises to what extent shall the Crown witnesses be cross-examined at the Preparatory. If the
cross-examination is directed to part only of the defence there is the danger, if the deposition be made
use of at the trial, that the prosecution may direct
attention to the fact that the cross-examination was
silent as to part of the defence, from which the inference may legitimately be drawn that the part on
which there is silence is an afterthought. What then
is the best course to pursue? I would advise cross-
examination on the witness's story, leaving out any
reference to the defence, and aiming simply at this:
to get as full and detailed facts as possible of *his*
story, so that at the trial you can obtain as many inconsistencies and contradictions as possible between
the story as told then and as told in the depositions.

CHAPTER XVII.

RE-EXAMINATION.

———

AN IMPRESSION appears to have been created among practitioners that the function of re-examination consists in the repetition of what the witness said in Examination in Chief: and such recapitulation only too often takes the form of the Practitioner putting the words into the witness's mouth. That is, he repeats what the witness has already said in the form of questions to which the latter answers "Yes" or "No" as required. Not only is this most contrary to the most elementary rules against putting leading questions, but it is mere waste of breath so far as any weight attaching to such a mode of examination is concerned. It should be apparent to the beginner that an answer elicited by a leading question cannot have the same weight attached to it as to one given without a suggestion being made by the practitioner examining the witness. But I would put it to him what weight can he imagine will possibly be attached to answers, where all the words are put into the witness's mouth by the Practitioner, and he answers "Yes" or "No" as required. Then consider the utter futility of such procedure. Either the witness has been "shaken" in what he said in Examination in Chief or he has not. If he has *not*, what is the sense of repeating it again? But if he has, then consider for a moment what the effect of such a mode of re-examination is. Suppose a witness has said in Chief that an incident took place on Friday, the day being material, and that in cross-examination it has been elicited from him that the events and incidents by which he fixes the day took place on a Thursday and not on a Friday; what does he consider the effect must be of the Practitioner rising to re-examine and saying, " You are sure you met X on the Friday," " You are sure that you saw him on the Friday, etc., etc.," repeating all the evidence deposed to in chief and making the witness swear positively that it was Friday. The effect can only be the impression that the witness is ready to swear to anything that will help his side.

It seems clear therefore that this mode of procedure cannot be one of the true functions of re-examination.

There is another and rather common procedure which is to be avoided. The Cross-examiner in striving to arrive at his objective and going cautiously, elicits answers which are unfavourable to him and therefore favourable to his opponent. Like a wise man he discontinues pursuing that line of examination. Now what happens over and over again is that the opponent on re-examination seizes on these favourable answers and tries to get the witness to " go one better." There is no mistaking what he is going to do from the moment he rises: there are signs of exultation all over him that now he has his adversary on the hip. Confidently he begins to get the witness to go still further than he has gone. Sometimes the latter does so: but sometimes he does not, and on the contrary begins to water down the force of his original replies. It may be asked, why should he do so? It is not always easy to diagnose the psychology of a witness: but it is a fact that witnesses do act in this way. The reason I am inclined to ascribe it to is, that when he is being cross-examined he is up in arms against the cross-examiner;

he knows that the latter is trying to break down his evidence and to tie him up into knots, so he is determined that he will not be bested. When, however, he returns to the more sympathetic atmosphere of " his own Counsel," he becomes calmer, reason once more assumes her sway, and he realizes that he has gone a little too far, with the result that he begins to correct his answers.

When this happens the re-examiner, especially if he is a beginner, gets deeper and deeper into the mire. His opponent begins to chuckle and manifest much glee. Instead of dropping the questioning at once, the beginner continues his re-examination, becomes irritated and determined to get the witness back to his original favourable answers—a hopeless task: and he only succeeds in making matters still worse.

It is always, I think, *bad advocacy to risk eliciting something unfavourable in the hope or expectation of obtaining a favourable answer.* This has been said several times: it cannot be too often emphasized by presenting it from various points of view.

The main and proper functions of re-examination would seem to be two-fold.

1. The one is *to endeavour to explain away the effects of a question or questions put in Cross-examination, and the answers thereto.*

2. *The other is to take advantage of every opportunity afforded by the cross-examination to put in evidence which but for the latter could not be put in.*

1.   RE-EXAMINATION BY WAY OF EXPLANATION.

The most obvious are those where the character of your witness is impeached, or motives, bias, prejudice, etc., on his part have been shown to exist, or have been suggested. If you have become acquainted with all the facts on these points which have been referred and alluded to by your opponent, you may be able to put some additional questions which will mitigate or reduce the bias, etc. If you have not the instructions or cannot put such questions, there does not seem to be any use in emphasizing and accentuating the bias, etc., by groping round in the hope that there may be something to be said in extenuation. Where suspicion merely has been aroused, the ground should be removed if possible. Again, quite an innocent act or admission, etc., may be made to look very prejudicial: if so, the true light should be thrown upon it.

What the practitioner should be very careful to watch for are "suggestions" of motives, bias and the like. When such attacks are made openly, they obtrude themselves and are obvious. But what may evade him are suggestions and hints as to motives and the like, which apparently insignificant may be made to assume somewhat alarming proportions in the address of a skilful practitioner. It is for these that a careful watch should be kept and the explanation elicited on re-examination.

2. RE-EXAMINATION SO AS TO GET IN EVIDENCE NOT ORIGINALLY ADMISSIBLE BUT WHICH THE CROSS-EXAMINER HAS LET IN.

This is only another application of the old story of profiting by your opponent's mistake. The Cross-examiner thinking that he will elicit something favourable has risked too much and has asked a question as to something which you in Chief could not ask. For example, a question as to a conversation at which your opponent's Client was not present. He may drop it like the proverbial "hot potato," but that is your opportunity. Having asked a question as to the contents of the conversation, you can now get the whole conversation in. This is a point upon which there is sure to be much wrangling and disputing. The Cross-examiner will contend strongly that what he asked does not let in anything more: it behoves the opposing practitioner therefore to be continually on the watch, so as to take advantage of every such opportunity.

Re-examination can only take place on something *which arises out of Cross-examination*: it is not a supplementary examination in Chief. Should the practitioner have forgotten to ask the witness something in Chief the proper course is to ask the Court to put the question to the witness. No doubt this request is often complied with by the Court allowing the practitioner to put the question himself: but there is no *right* to do so, it can only be done through the Court.

CHAPTER XVIII.

THE ADDRESS ON THE FACTS.

I TAKE it that in the art of speaking as in all other
arts the true key-note to conviction is sincerity. No
matter how dull or uninteresting the subject matter
of the facts, or how monotonous the speaker may be,
his address cannot fail to be listened to, if he be sin-
cere. Mere facility or fluency, etc., never has the same
force. There are speakers who by " the exuberance of
their own verbosity " talk themselves into the belief
of the righteousness of the Client's cause, when they
know better: but although they may convince themselves by these means, they fail to convince their
hearers.

The class of case, however, which falls to the young
practitioner is not such as to admit of much scope:
they are generally sordid and common-place, accompanied by brutality and coarseness. Something else
is, therefore, required than the placing of reliance on
the natural ability of the speaker. In other words, he
must learn how to use his voice. It would, of course,
be comparatively easy to fill pages with advice and
suggestions on an address to a Jury: but it would
not be of the very least practical use. The practitioner might as well try to learn singing from a
theoretical treatise without exercises. He must have
practical teaching in the use of his voice: teaching
that should not be confined to poems such as " The

Charge of the Light Brigade," etc., but should include the delivery of speeches: not the oratorical flights, polished and elaborated by successive editors and assigned to such speakers as Burke, but the more common-place and everyday addresses, such as Bright's—speeches much more difficult to deal with, but of much greater utility in training, than those burning with eloquence. If the practitioner is defending Klaas Geswint, charged with stealing a sheep, the model of an oration on the Natural Rights of man will not be of much use to him. But what he can learn is how to use his voice by some practical teaching.

There is one point, however, which seems to me to merit a few words. It is somewhat remarkable that in the appeals so constantly made to Juries, so little emotion is ever shown by the speaker. It is not suggested that the kind of demonstrative feeling should be displayed which one may see in the Courts of more emotional races. There is no need to sob or weep. But it is surely the greatest mistake possible to suppose that an ordinary Jury is not susceptible to emotional feeling. One has but to go to a Theatre, and note the emotion displayed, especially in a trial case, when the Defending Counsel puts some feeling into his words. Of course, they must ring true: if not, the result is more likely to be bathos than pathos. For the beginner there is not as a rule much opportunity for showing feeling. When Piet Dragoender is charged with a serious assault, the ordinary consequence of a Saturday afternoon drink, it would be the height of absurdity to attempt to influence the result by any display of emotion. Still such opportunities do occur sometimes, to a very slight degree it is true, though just sufficient to allow of a suggestion of emotion: and if this is imparted to the Jury, they, being human, will be much more attuned to taking the view of the facts put before them on behalf of the Accused: but whether it is from the natural racial reserve or from a fear of making "an ass of oneself," they are seldom, if ever, made use of.

———————

Chapter XIX.

PROCEDURE UNKNOWN TO THE BARRISTER.

———

THERE ARE some everyday matters of practice in our Courts which are quite novel to the Practitioner who has qualified out of South Africa. It may be of some assistance to him to indicate what the procedure is in such cases, however well known they may be to the South African practitioner.

A. ARREST AD FIRMANDEM JURISDICTIONEM.

This is often spoken of, but incorrectly, as arrest ad fundandam jurisdictionem. as if the arrest created a jurisdiction which the Court does not otherwise possess.

It has been decided in the Cape Province that the Court has jurisdiction on three grounds:

(1) by reason of the Defendant being domiciled within the territorial limits of its jurisdiction (the forum domicilii) :

(2) by virtue of the contract having been entered into or having to be performed within such limits (the forum contractus) :

(3) by virtue of the subject matter in an action in rem being situated within such limits (the forum rei sitae).

If the Defendant is domiciled here then no arrest is necessary. But if the Defendant is not, and the

Court has jurisdiction under one of the above heads, then the practice is, that before an action against the Defendant is commenced, the Court must be moved for the arrest of the Defendant, if he be within such aforesaid limits, or for the arrest of some property belonging to the Defendant, and situated within such limits, for the purpose of "founding jurisdiction," as it is sometimes called, or of "confirming jurisdiction."

But be it noted that it has been decided in the Cape Province that the Court will not grant such arrest for the purpose of *creating* the jurisdiction: such jurisdiction *must exist* under one of the above heads before the arrest will be granted.

B.   CONFIRMATION OF AN ACCOUNT IN AN INSOLVENT ESTATE.

Counsel simply moves for the confirmation of such account. Nothing more is required or necessary. If the motion is opposed, then the procedure is all based on affidavits, which raise the points in issue.

C.   DIVORCE ACTIONS.

A divorce is generally obtained on one of the following grounds: (a) Adultery; (b) Malicious desertion.

In the former case the Plaintiff usually prays not only for a decree of divorce but also for "*forfeiture of benefits.*" The meaning of this is that the guilty party may be ordered to forfeit all benefits which he or she *has derived from the innocent party* by reason of the marriage. Thus, if the husband has settled any property on his wife by antenuptial contract, and the latter is the guilty party, she may be ordered to forfeit such settlement. Again, where the parties are married in community of property and a forfeiture is decreed, then the guilty party can only *take* that which he (or she) *brought into the marriage*. He (or she) does not forfeit his *own* property: but only all share or benefit, which he was, by virtue of the community, entitled to, in the property of the *innocent* party.

In the latter case, viz.: *Malicious Desertion,* the Plaintiff, after alleging the marriage, states in his declaration that the Defendant has wrongfully and *maliciously* deserted the Plaintiff. In his prayer he claims:

(a) that the Defendant be ordered to return to and cohabit with the Plaintiff, or shortly for " An order for Restitution of Conjugal rights." *But he also proceeds to add the following prayers*: viz., " Failing compliance with the said order, he prays

(b) for a decree of divorce.

(c) Custody of the children.

(d) Forfeiture of benefits arising from the community or under the antenuptial contract, etc., as the case may be.

(e) Costs of suit.

If the Court grants the order of Restitution of Conjugal Rights, the following is then the procedure. The Court orders the Defendant to restore Conjugal Rights by a certain fixed day, failing which to show cause on a later fixed day why the order should not be granted as prayed for in prayers (b), (c), (d) and (e). On the arrival of the lastmentioned return day, if the Defendant has not complied with the order of restitution, the Plaintiff files an affidavit to the effect that the Defendant has not returned to and cohabited with the Plaintiff by the firstmentioned date.

Where the parties have been married in community and a forfeiture is decreed, Counsel should ask the

Court to appoint some person or persons to divide the joint estate of the parties, and should be prepared with the name of some fit person to be so appointed.

D.   EDICTAL CITATION—FILING INTENDIT.

Where the Defendant is within the Court's jurisdiction, but cannot be served with a summons in the ordinary way, for example, if his whereabouts are unknown, although there is reason to believe that he is within the jurisdiction, *or* where he cannot be found, *or* where he is himself unknown, as for example where the Defendants are heirs ab intestato, and the Plaintiff does not know who are the heirs ab intestato, *or* where the Defendant is out of the jurisdiction of the Court, and there is no one within the jurisdiction authorized to accept service, then application must be made to the Court for leave to sue by *Edictal Citation*. This means no more than that the Court gives directions as to the mode in which the *summons* is to be served. Such directions usually include, as an alternative to personal service, publication in some newspaper circulating in the place where the Defendant resided or was last heard of. So that Counsel should be prepared with the names of such newspapers. He should also be prepared with information as to the length of time required to elapse before the return day, which is fixed when such directions are given.

The "intendit" means no more than the Declaration. Wherever an "intendit" or declaration is necessary, Counsel applies, at the same time when asking for leave to sue by Edictal Citation, for leave to *file also the intendit*. *i.e.*, to file the declaration, and *to serve the notice to plead* : and also to *serve the notice of trial*.

E. INTERDICTS.

As the young practitioner may find the cases and authorities on interdicts somewhat confusing, it will be well for him to follow the principles as laid down by *Innes, C.J.*, in *Settogelo* v. *Settogelo* (1911 A.D. 227).

They amount to these:—

1. Where an applicant can show a *clear right* he may apply for an Interdict.
BUT

2. Where the right is *not* shown to be a clear one, but the right asserted, though *prima facie* established, is open to some doubt, then the applicant must show that the injury feared is *irreparable*.

F. JUDGMENT UNDER RULE /319.

Where a Defendant is barred from pleading in an action for *a debt* or *liquidated demand*, Counsel is often briefed to pray for Judgment under rule 319, and he does so upon the prayer of the declaration. It is well in such a case to consult the decisions in order to ascertain what has been held to be a "liquidated demand." It has been decided for example that a prayer for cancellation of a lease is such a demand.

G. PRO DEO OR PAUPER SUITS OR IN FORMA PAUPERIS SUITS.

Every person not possessed of £10 (excepting household goods, wearing apparel, tools of trade, and the matter or thing claimed in the suit) may apply to the Court for leave to sue or defend as a pauper. The application must be supported by the affidavit of two householders, living in his neighbourhood, that he is not so possessed of property to the value of £10.

On Counsel moving for such leave, the petitioner must be present in Court for the purpose of being examined as to his means. If he live at any distance from the seat of the Court, the latter generally refers the enquiry to the Magistrate of the District, in which the petitioner lives, for his report, and on the return of his report the application is renewed.

If such leave is granted, the Court refers the matter to the Counsel moving for his " certificate of probable cause." Thereupon it is the duty of such Counsel to enquire into the case and satisfy himself that the Applicant has a probable cause of action or defence. If so satisfied, he endorses on the application " I certify probabilis causa."

An improper practice has grown up of Counsel making such enquiry *before* the Court has granted the leave, that is before the Court is satisfied that the Applicant should be allowed to sue or defend as a pauper. This becomes apparent when the Court refers the matter to Counsel for his Certificate, and the latter thereupon says " I am prepared now to certify," showing that he has already made the enquiry. But *until* the Court has granted the leave and has *requested* Counsel to certify, no Counsel should make such enquiry.

Counsel then moves the Court for a rule nisi, calling on the opposite party to show cause why the applicant should not sue or defend in forma pauperis. If the opposite party opposes, he files affidavits, to which the applicant may reply.

If the Rule nisi is made absolute, then the Court appoints Counsel and Attorney for the Applicant, and the action proceeds in the usual way.

No such Counsel or Attorney may charge or take any fees, but if the applicant (i.e., the pauper) wins his case and costs are awarded against the opposite side, then both such Counsel and Attorney for the Pauper are entitled to and shall receive " all such fees as are allowed on taxation."

NAMPTISSEMENT OR PROVISIONAL JUDGMENT.

This means a provisional or interlocutory Judgment, granted on the production of a " liquid document," upon the plaintiff giving security (de restituendo) to restore the amount paid to him or received in execution, should it be found on the action being tried on its merits (known as the *" principle case "*) that the Plaintiff was not entitled to the debt claimed.

A liquid document is a written undertaking or acknowledgment of debt signed by the debtor, showing on the face of it, without the aid of any further other evidence, a debt then due and owing and liquidated. Thus a mortgage bond, or a promissory note, or an I.O.U. or a lease stipulating for a fixed rent, are all documents which on the face of them show a liquidated debt, due and owing. But a promise to a Hospital to pay 5/- a day " so long as the debtor shall be treated as a patient therein " is not such a document: because in order to ascertain what amount is due, evidence would be required to show how many days the patient was treated in the Hospital. In the same way any document which makes the indebtness dependent on a condition is not a liquid document, because evidence would be required to prove that the condition had been performed.

Counsel moves for " Provisional sentence," and at the same time hands into Court the original document on which the claim is founded.

The claim may be opposed, and the opposition is generally either upon the merits of the indebtedness or by way of denial of the signature to the document.

In the former case the procedure is upon affidavit.

"Provisional Sentence" may be refused, and the Plaintiff ordered to go into the "Principal Case": that is, the Plaintiff files a declaration and proceeds in the ordinary way of action.

In the latter case, the Court fixes a day for the trial of the issue, viz., whether or not the signature is that of the Defendant. On that day witnesses are examined viva voce as in any other action in which witnesses are examined: but only upon that one issue of fact, viz., the signature of the Defendant.

I. REHABILITATION.

As it is provided by the Insolvent Act, number 32 of 1916, that the provisions of the repealed Statutes (in the Cape Province, Ordinance 6 of 1843 and Act number 38 of 1884) shall continue to be applicable to any estate sequestrated or assigned at the commencement of the Act, viz.: January the 1st, 1917, the different kinds of applications for the rehabilitation or discharge of an Insolvent may prove somewhat puzzling to the beginner. The requisites, therefore, of such applications, both in the Cape Province under the repealed Statutes, and under the Act 32 of 1917 are here given. And the practitioner is recommended to draw up similarly for himself the various applications under the repealed Statutes in the other Provinces.

IN THE CAPE PROVINCE IN THE CASE OF AN ESTATE SEQUESTRATED BEFORE THE 1ST OF JANUARY, 1917.

1. REHABILITATION UNDER SECTION 117 OF ORDINANCE 6 OF 1843.

> A. The requisites are: (1) Notice of application with proof of service on the Trustee: (2) Master's Certificate that *four-fifths* in number and value of Creditors consent.

or B. After six months from confirmation of plan of distribution, then the requisites are: *either* Consent of three-fifths in number and value of creditors, *or* (2) Consent of nine-tenths in value alone of Creditors.

DISCHARGE.

1. UNDER SECTION 106 OF ORDINANCE 6 OF 1843.

   The requisites are:

   1. Notice of the application with proof of service on the Trustee:
   2. The Master's Certificate that an *offer of composition* has been accepted by *four-fifths* in number and value of the Creditors.
   3. Affidavit of full and fair surrender.
   4. Twenty-one days' notice in the *Gazette*.
   5. Deposit of £25 security to the satisfaction of the Master or Magistrate of the District.
   6. Where the papers do not disclose who the Trustee is a Certificate of the Trustee's appointment.

2. UNDER ACT 38 OF 1884, SECTION 14, SUBSECTION 1.

   If the Insolvent has not been convicted of fraudulent Insolvency, the Court may, after *four years* from the date of the surrender or sequestration, order his discharge without any consent of the creditors.

   The requisites are:

   1. Affidavit of full and fair surrender.
   2. Six months' notice in the *Gazette*.
   3. Security for £25 to the satisfaction of the Master or Magistrate of the District.
   4. Idem as Number 6 last-mentioned.

RELEASE.

1. UNDER SECTION 107 OF ORDINANCE NUMBER 6 OF 1843 AFTER THE 3RD MEETING.

The requisites are:

1. Notice of application with proof of Service on Trustee.

2. The Master's Certificate that all the Creditors consent to the release of the Insolvent or that the Creditors have been paid in full.

3. Twenty-one days' notice in the *Gazette*. (The Court has not required this where *all the Creditors*, both those who have proved and those who have not, have consented.)

RELEASE, GENERAL.

It is an established practice that on the production of the Master's Certificate that no Creditors have appeared at the meeting and that no Trustee has been elected, the Court, upon proof of notice of the application in the *Gazette*, will grant an order of release.

REHABILITATION UNDER ACT NUMBER 32 OF 1916.

1. ON AN OFFER OF COMPOSITION (Under Section 108, Subsection 1).

The requisites are:

1. Notice of application and proof of service on Trustee.

2. Affidavit of full and fair surrender: "(Section 110)".

3. Security for £25 to the Satisfaction of the *Registrar*.

4. Three weeks' notice in the *Gazette*.

    5.   Insolvent to set out particulars of offer of composition.

2. AFTER EXPIRATION OF SIX MONTHS FROM DATE OF CONFIRMATION OF ANY LIQUIDATION AND DISTRIBUTION ACCOUNT.

    1, 2, and 3 same as last mentioned.

    4.   Six months' notice in *Gazette* and in writing to Master and Trustee.

3. WHERE NO CLAIM PROVED AND NO TRUSTEE APPOINTED (Section 108, Subsection 3) AFTER 6 MONTHS FROM DATE OF SEQUESTRATION.

    1 and 2 same as before.

    3.   Six weeks' notice in *Gazette*.

    4.   Notice in writing to Master and Trustee.

Under Section 111, Subsection 1, the Master must report on applications.

J. SEQUESTRATION AND CONSIGNATION.

There are two remedies (though termed contracts by Van der Linden) in our Law known respectively as *Sequestration* and *Consignation*.

This *Sequestration* has nothing to do with the sequestration of an Insolvent estate, but means the taking care of any property, which is in dispute, by a third party, appointed by agreement or by the Court, to be handed over to the one who, on the dispute being decided, is declared to be entitled to such property.

Consignation consists in the receipt and taking care of moneys, of which the true owner is uncertain.

For fuller information on these remedies the practitioner is referred to Van der Linden's Institutes, 1.15.6.

K. " WRIT OF SPOLIATION."

Where a person has been forcibly or secretly dispossessed or deprived of any property, application may be made to the Court for a Writ (or Mandamus) of *Spoliation*, ordering the applicant to be replaced in possession of the property from which he has been so forcibly or secretly dispossessed, or ordering the restoration of the property of which he has been in like manner deprived.

The basis or principle upon which this remedy has been founded is " spoliatus ante omnia restituendus est," and therefore the Respondent in such an application *cannot set up any defence upon the merits*: he cannot enter at all into the question whether or not he was entitled to the possession or to the property. The sole issue or question involved is whether or not he forcibly or secretly dispossessed or deprived the applicant of the property. If he has, then he must restore the possession or property. The question of his rights he can raise in the proper legal manner after he has made restitution.

CHAPTER XX.

RELATIONS BETWEEN BENCH AND PRACTITIONER.

———

QUESTIONS OF proprietory conduct affecting the relation of the Bench and the practitioner, or in the conduct of a case sometimes arise. Wherever possible, it is a wise thing to consult some of the leaders of the Bar as to what is the proper course to pursue. No doubt there are questions upon which different opinions may be held. Thus the practitioner may be briefed to defend an Accused charged with a crime, and facts may come to his knowledge which *prove* that the Accused is guilty: should the practitioner continue to hold the brief?

That depends on the circumstances. He certainly would not continue to hold the Brief if that meant that he was to listen to the Accused or his witnesses stating in the witness-box what he knew was not the case. Or again, suppose in the conduct of a case facts come to his knowledge which, if not made known, would lead the statements made by his Client or the latter's witnesses to mislead or deceive the Court. He would certainly refuse to be a party to such misleading or deception. Such cases are clear.

E converso it is also clear that there can be no objection to his holding the Brief where it is a question whether the facts do or do not amount in Law to the crime charged. Thus a man may be charged with murder and he may admit that he killed the deceased: it does not follow that the killing amounts to murder, and there is no reason why the practitioner should not conduct the case with a view to reducing the crime either to one of manslaughter or of justifiable homicide—provided always that neither of the deterrent elements abovementioned are introduced.

In these respects there cannot I conceive be any difference of opinion. The question arises in cases other than the above. There are good men who hold that so long as neither of the deterrent elements are introduced, Counsel is entitled to do everything in the conduct of a defence which may go to show mitigation or provocation or reduce the aggravation.

It is the application of the latter of the abovementioned deterrent elements which makes it the duty of a practitioner who has granted a Certificate of Probabilis causa to withdraw that certificate if facts come to his knowledge, which if known to him at the time when he granted the Certificate would have induced him to refuse to certify.

Where a matter is undefended, and the practitioner is aware of a prior decision against him, he should bring it to the notice of the Court, and endeavour to distinguish it.

It sometimes becomes a question whether Counsel should argue for a position or on a point on which the Law *is clearly against him*. That depends first of all upon the words in italics. In the case of *Hunter's Trustees* v. *the Colonial Government* (4 J. 449) the Counsel for *Plaintiffs* declined to take up the time of the Court in argument as he stated that the Law was clearly *against* him: thereupon Counsel for the Defendant was called upon, and after hearing him the Court gave Judgment *for the Plaintiffs*.

There can, however, be no doubt that it is bad advocacy to labour untenable points, or to treat all the questions of varying importance that arise in argument as if they were all equally important or matters of life and death. But even here it may be asked *when is a point untenable?*

In the first appeal that fell to me, I took one point among others. The late Chief Justice threw down his pen and asked me whether I was serious. I stuck to it, however, and eventually the Court held that that was *the only* point in the case.

Every practitioner soon learns, however, that there are questions of varying degrees of weight in a case, and when he has made up his mind as to their importance should not labour them all as if no difference existed. Certainly, the practitioner who is strong enough to discriminate is he who will gain the desired reputation and will get on in his profession.

INDEX.

Lightning Source UK Ltd.
Milton Keynes UK
UKOW07f1336300717

306274UK00003B/23/P

9 781289 356514